Bullying in American Schools

ALSO BY ANNE G. GARRETT

Keeping American Schools Safe:
A Handbook for Parents, Students, Educators,
Law Enforcement Personnel and the Community
(McFarland, 2001)

Bullying in American Schools

Causes, Preventions, Interventions

ANNE G. GARRETT

McFarland & Company, Inc., Publishers
Jefferson, North Carolina, and London

Library of Congress Cataloguing-in-Publication Data

Garrett, Anne G.
    Bullying in American schools : causes, preventions,
    interventions / Anne G. Garrett
        p.   cm.
    Includes bibliographical references and index.

    ISBN 0-7864-1549-5 (softcover : 50# alkaline paper) ∞

    1. Bullying in schools— United States.   2. Bullying in
    schools— United States— Prevention.   I. Title.
    LB3013.32.G37   2003   2003001401
    371.5'8 — dc21

British Library cataloguing data are available

Manufactured in the United States of America

Cover photograph ©2002 PhotoDisc

McFarland & Company, Inc., Publishers
    Box 611, Jefferson, North Carolina 28640
    www.mcfarlandpub.com

To the victims of bullies—
there's someone out there who can help you—just ask.

To the bullies—let's stop this behavior.
Working together, we can make a difference.

Contents

Introduction

Most school violence begins with bullying. Serious school violence starts with seemingly innocent bullying or put-downs that eventually escalate into violence involving guns or knives. The lack of respect for another person's rights, the most common factor in all criminal behaviors, begins with bullying. Schools are a breeding ground for this criminal behavior, which poses a serious threat to the public if it is not addressed when it first appears. It is possible to identify bullying behavior as early as pre-school or kindergarten. Educators can tell who the bullies are within the first ten days of each school year.

Since 1992, there have been 250 violent deaths in schools that involved multiple victims, including the horrid Columbine High School massacre. In virtually every school shooting, bullying has been a factor. As in the Littleton, Colorado, shootings, most of the students who committed these violent crimes were victims of bullying who finally decided to get revenge.

We must learn from the Columbine massacre if we are to prevent it from happening again. The group of Columbine students identified as the "trench coat mafia," which included Eric Harris and Dylan Klebold, was harassed, bullied and put down on a daily basis for years. This was initiated by a clique of student athletes and later joined by many other Columbine students. Every day when Harris and Klebold came to school, they were met at the door by a gauntlet of students that harassed them by pouring orange juice on their trench coats so they would have to wear the sticky stuff all day. Harris and Klebold and others in this group who were bullied tried to sneak into school through a side door or back door to avoid this daily ritual. They were also harassed and called names in the hallways and cafeteria.

As they opened fire into the classrooms on April 20, 1999, Harris and Klebold were heard to say, "This is for all the people who made fun of us all these years" (Dube, 1999). Even with their obvious cries for help, no one gave them the kind of attention they really needed. These boys were very bright and lonely and yet no one seemed to try to redirect their behavior in more positive ways. Cliques like these that bullied Harris and Klebold at Columbine High School exist in every school in the world.

Though bullies have been around since the days of the one-room schoolhouse, they're more vicious today and the consequences are more deadly—they are a major cause of shootings and suicides.

However it is defined, bullying is not just child's play, but a terrifying experience many schoolchildren face every day. It can be as direct as teasing, hitting or threatening, or as indirect as exclusions, rumors or manipulation. During the past decade, bullying has become more lethal and has occurred more frequently than it has in the previous two decades. In our quest to provide the quality education that our children deserve, this problem can no longer be treated lightly.

Chapter One defines bullying as a form of violence among children. This form of behavior often occurs in the presence of adults and has been considered by some adults as uncontrollable and a normal part of growing up. In this chapter, characteristics of a bully will be provided and a profile developed. Also, staggering research on bullies will be presented.

Chapter Two identifies myths about bullies and examines research that dispels the myths. Much of what we have been studying for the last 30 years is wrong. Consequently, many of our techniques for dealing with bullies and their victims have simply made the problem worse.

Chapter Three tells how school violence begins with bullying. Serious violence that involves lethal weapons can begin with seemingly benign bullying or put-downs and escalate from there. School bullying is often the first manifestation of the lack of respect for another person's rights, a common denominator of all criminal behavior.

Chapter Four identifies the perpetrator's behavior as not existing in isolation. Rather, it may indicate the beginning of a generally antisocial and rule-breaking behavior pattern that can extend into adulthood. Successful programs and interventions will be shared with the reader.

Chapter Five will provide useful solutions and strategies. Now is the time to stop this. In the wake of school shootings and violence that our children are beginning to experience, we need to make serious changes. Instead of ignoring the problem, let's become proactive and start taking control of the situation. How do we do this? This solution section is provided for government officials, board of education members, law enforcement officials, school administrators and teachers, students, parents and the community.

One

What Is Bullying?

There is some confusion as to what constitutes bullying. Bullying is not easy to define. Sometimes it involves hitting or kicking. It may be passive, as in rumors, exclusion or manipulation. But threats, teasing and taunting are more common and can be more damaging. However it is defined, bullying cannot be dismissed as child's play. It can be a humiliating or terrifying experience, and at its worst can lead to violence. It deserves serious attention. Bullying can no longer be explained away, as some adults have done in the past, as a normal part of growing up. For many years, bullying was seen as a necessary evil — an unpleasant but unavoidable rite of childhood. Ignore it, we thought, and it too shall pass. The problem hasn't gone away, though, and many educators and parents can no longer avoid it. Bullying has only harmful, and certainly no beneficial, effects for the target, the perpetrator, and even the bystander.

Bullying and teasing top the list of children's school troubles. The pain brought about by taunts and threats at school appears to have played a role in recent fatal school shootings— evidence that this unrelieved stress may explode into tragedy. More than two-thirds of school shooters said they felt persecuted or bullied by other students. The motive for the shootings was often revenge. The National School Safety Center agrees that bullying is the most enduring and underrated problem in American schools today.

Bullying can also be defined as unwanted words or physical actions that can make a person feel bad. This behavior is generally distinguished from good-natured teasing by the way the recipient feels. Children who are teased are not made to feel bad because it is clear that the behavior is done for fun.

Many children in our nation's schools are robbed of their opportunity to learn because they are bullied and victimized daily. Bullying exacts a terrible toll on children, and the scars can last a lifetime. The word "bully" is used to describe many different types of behavior ranging from teasing or deliberately leaving an individual out of a school gathering or ignoring them to serious assaults and abuse. Sometimes it is an individual who is doing the bullying and sometimes it is a group. The important thing is not the action but the effect on the victim. No one should ever underestimate the fear that a bullied child feels. Bullying can also be defined as something that someone repeatedly does or says to gain power over or to dominate another individual. Bullying is where a child or group of children keep taking advantage of the power they have to hurt or reject someone else. Some of the ways children bully another child include: calling them names, saying or writing nasty comments about them, leaving them out of activities or not talking to them, threatening them, or making them feel uncomfortable or scared, stealing or damaging their belongings, hitting or kicking them, or making them do things they don't want to do.

——— *A Serious Problem for Kids* ———

Bullying behavior may seem insignificant compared to kids bringing guns to school or getting involved with drugs. Bullying is often dismissed as part of growing up. But it can be an early form of aggressive, violent behavior. One of four children who bully will have a criminal record by the age of 30.

Bullies often cause serious problems that schools, families and neighbors ignore. Teasing at bus stops, taking another child's lunch money, insults and threats, kicking or shoving — it's all a game for the bully. Fears and anxieties about bullies can cause some children to avoid school, carry a gun or knife for protection or even commit a violent act.

Although anyone can be the target of bullying behavior, the victim is often singled out because of his or her psychological traits more than his or her physical traits. A typical victim is likely to be shy, sensitive and perhaps anxious or insecure. Some children are picked on for physical reasons such as being overweight or physically small, having a disability, or belonging to a different race or religion.

Bullying, a form of abuse and sometimes violence among children, is common on school playgrounds, in neighborhoods, and in homes throughout the world. Often occurring out of the presence of adults or in front of adults who fail to intercede, bullying has long been considered an inevitable end and, in some ways, an uncontrollable part of growing up. School bullying has come under intense public and media scrutiny recently amid reports that it may have been a contributing factor in shootings at Columbine High School in Littleton, Colorado, in 1999, at Santana High School in Santee, California, in early 2001, and in other acts of juvenile violence, including suicide. Bullying can affect the social environment of a school, creating a climate of fear among students, inhibiting their ability to learn, and leading to other antisocial behavior. Through research and evaluation, successful programs to recognize, prevent, and effectively intervene in bullying behavior have been developed and replicated in schools across the country. (These strategies and programs will be discussed in Chapter Four.)

Bullying and being bullied appear to be important indicators that something is wrong. Children who experience either or both need help. In light of the recent shootings, parents and educators have become concerned about whether bullying behavior or being the victim may contribute to more serious acts of aggression. Experts disagree about predicting future violent behavior from earlier bullying tendencies. Aggression is a very stable trait and can be long lasting. There is some correlation between behavior and later violence, but research is uncertain how strong it is. One commonly cited British study reported that individuals with a history of bullying had a fourfold increase in criminal behavior by the age of 24. The British study, however, examined only violent behaviors—such as beating up someone after school, and not the minor offenses such as name calling. Recently, the Secret Service attempted to create a profile of a child who acts out with gun violence, and found that a student's tendency to become a school shooter cannot be predicted based on involvement in bullying activities. Poor academic performance and psychological disorders were not indicators of potential violent behavior. This was very disturbing to educators. As educators, we see these children every day, not just for interviewing purposes, and we know if certain students have violent tendencies, based upon bullying activities that have taken place in our schools.

Bill Bond, principal at West Paducah High in 1997, told ABC News reporter Oliver Yates Libaw that taunting or teasing could not begin to justify Michael Carneal's deadly rampage at the school which left 14 year old Brian Zuckor and 15 year old Randy Gordon dead and 13 others injured. He further elaborated that taking bullying seriously is a key to preventing school shootings and other acts of student violence. "In almost every case, they have been bullied" Bond said (Libaw, 2001). Bond believes there is less hazing and harassment at schools today than 10 or 20 years ago, but he still thinks this is an area that needs improvement. The rash of school shootings in recent years has made it even more vital to deal with the problem, he says.

Authorities say a planned massacre at a New Bedford, Mass., high school could have been another Columbine or perhaps even worse — if police had not gotten word that a group of students may have been plotting to detonate explosives, shoot classmates and then kill themselves. The students pleaded not guilty, but according to police reports, the five teens who allegedly planned the attack had complained of being picked on and called names. A note found by the janitor at the school spoke of "getting everyone back for calling us names and beating us with ugly sticks" (ABC News, November 28, 2001). This statement brings back fearful memories of Eric Harris, one of the attackers at Columbine High in Littleton, Colorado. He accused other students of ridiculing him, not accepting him, and not being worth their time; he vowed to seek revenge and kill them. According to the ABC News commentary, "Serious Bullying" (November 28, 2001), bullying is a serious and widespread problem that can lead to school shootings and suicide. At the same time, it is dangerously underrated; adults and schools are not taking the problem seriously enough.

In the United States alone, 269 students, teachers and support personnel died in school related violence between September 1992 and May 2000. As shocking as that statistic is, those deaths represent only a small percentage of thousands of violent acts that occur each year in our nation's schools. Although no single causation factor has been identified, experts point to a number of contributing factors common among children who display violent behavior. According to Sylvia Rimm, author of *Why Kids Kill: Exploring the Causes and Possible Solutions* (Education World, 2000), children who have expressed anger and violent behavior have been teased or bullied by others.

Defining Bullying

A principal in North Carolina witnessed two fifth grade boys in the bathroom bullying a first grade student. One of the fifth graders was holding him and the other one was yelling in his face that he was going to beat him to a bloody pulp. The principal had the three boys come to her office. After extensively interviewing the boys, the principal found that the fifth graders did not see anything wrong with their behavior. Meanwhile, the first grade student was crying and extremely terrified. The principal called the parents of each of the boys. One of the fifth grade parents did not see that her child had done anything wrong. The second parent of the fifth grader demanded that her son apologize and be justly punished. The parent of the first grade child wanted to call the police because her child had been assaulted. The principal gave just punishment to the two fifth grade students and advised counseling for the first grader. Bullying can be systematically and chronically inflicting physical hurt or psychological distress on one or more students. In this situation, the first grader was traumatized psychologically, but if the principal had not entered the restroom, there is a great possibility that he would have been physically assaulted.

According to Dan Olweus, a psychology professor at Norway's University of Bergen and one of the world's leading experts on bullies and their victims, bullying is an accumulation of negative reactions—occurring repeatedly and over a period of time—directed toward one student by another student or students. Those negative actions, which can include threats, physical attacks, words, gestures, or social exclusion, occur in a context always characterized by an imbalance between the bully and the victim. The repercussions of bullying, even when it doesn't escalate into violence, are rarely limited to the victims alone. Olweus states that students in schools with serious bullying problems report feeling less safe and less satisfied with their schools. Students in schools where bullying problems are ignored and aggressive behavior is not addressed are likely to become more aggressive and less tolerant as well. Bullying affects the school climate and the learning environment of every classroom.

It's important to know the difference between normal peer conflict and bullying. Normal peer conflict is when two students of equal status and power get into an argument or a fight, but it's more accidental, and not serious. In the bullying incident, you have a balance of power and the students are not friends. The bullying is repeated, and the bully is seeking to gain power and control over the victim.

Glenn Stutzky, a school violence specialist with the School of Social Work at Michigan State University, was interviewed for ABC News in 2000. In the interview, Stutzky defined a bully as an individual who seeks to control, dominate and terrorize the life of another. The essence of bullying is about power — an imbalance and an abuse of power.

Bullying among children encompasses a variety of negative acts carried out repeatedly over a period of time. It involves a real or perceived imbalance of power, with the more powerful child or group attacking those who are less powerful. Bullying is a relationship and goes beyond individual incidents which by themselves can seem petty and insignificant, but bring great pain and torment to the victims. The dynamics of violence and school playground bullying are very similar. It is an issue of power. The essence of bullying is not in the actions of the bully but in his or her intentions. Will they bring harm? Is there intention to control? Bullying is deeply embedded in our culture. There are bullies not only on the school playgrounds but bullies who are board chairpersons, university presidents, politicians, pastors, teachers, police chiefs, rabbis and clerics. And bullying has achieved results in the sense of increasing profits, domination of markets and maintaining positions of power. Bullying tactics are routinely used in both the public and private sector.

Home Environment

Bullies are produced in the home, shaped by a combination of factors, including lack of parental warmth and attention, poor supervision, parental modeling of aggressive behavior, and an active and impulsive temperament on the part of the child. The victims of bullies are most often created at the school. As with alcoholism and other forms of abusive behavior, bullying tends to be an intergenerated problem. Many childhood bullies are often abused at home by a parent and witness that parent abusing his spouse and the child's siblings. A bully at school is a bully at home. Living with abusive parents teaches children that aggression and violence are effective and appropriate means to attain a goal.

Gender

A recent study (Olweus and Limber, 1999), found that males tend to bully and be bullied more frequently than females. For males, physical and verbal bullying is most common; for females, verbal bullying (both taunting and insults of a sexual nature) and spreading rumors are more common. Bullying generally begins in the elementary grades, peaks in the sixth through the eighth grades, and persists into high school.

Research has suggested that boys and girls experience bullying in a different manner. Boys tend to experience more physical aggression than girls, and are more likely to be the target. This gender difference is evident in elementary as well as middle school. A difference in the type of bullying has also been found, as males tend to be more physical than females and females are more likely to use relational aggression — such as excluding one from social gatherings. It has been reported that girls have more negative views on bullying than do boys (Walsh, 2001).

Characteristics of bullies

When identifying characteristics of bullies, we can never be sure how accurate they are or that we are not stereotyping. No one symptom stands out to label a bully. As educators, parents and community members, we must observe our children for certain traits. In this way we can establish whether there is a pattern of mild, moderate or severe levels of bullying. We can increase our ability to recognize early warning signs by establishing close, caring and supportive relationships with children and youth. We can insure these behaviors are not misinterpreted by using several significant principles to better understand them. Bullies tend to do one or more of the following:

- Harass or intimidate others, both verbally and nonverbally;
- Call other children names;
- If they are boys, bully more often and use more physical means;
- If they are girls, use more subtle means such as whispering about others, spreading rumors and shunning their victims; and
- Perpetrate bullying in and around school, where normally an audience is available.

Research Findings

Research on peer victimization in schools has increased dramatically in recent years. This is a critical issue because it is so prevalent, and because it has long-lasting consequences. A convincing case can be made for the negative social, academic, psychological, and physical impact of bullying in the schools and communities. Exposure to bullying by peers has been found to be related to increased dropout rates, lower self-esteem, fewer friends, declining grades, and increases in illnesses. Bullies in elementary and middle school are more likely to be convicted of crimes and more likely to take part in sexual harassment and assault in high school and in adulthood. The period of transition between elementary and middle school is critical and has been referred to as brutal due to the increased frequency and intensity of aggression experienced by students (Walsh, 2001).

Research on bullying in schools has shown:

- 10 percent of high school dropouts do so because of repeat bullying (Weinhold & Weinhold, 1998).
- 20 percent of all high school students surveyed reported they avoid the restrooms out of fear of being bullied (National Institute for Dispute Resolution [NIDR], 1999).
- In the U.S., 270,000 students carry guns to school each day to protect themselves (Garrett, 2001).
- Younger children, grades six to ten, are more likely to be victims of violence in schools than senior high school students (Garrett, 2001).
- Nearly one-third of students have heard a classmate threaten to kill someone (Langer, 1999).
- 78 percent of those who knew of the threats said they didn't report them to an adult (Langer, 1999).
- 40 percent of high school students say there are potentially violent cliques in their school (Langer, 1999).
- One in five say they personally know a classmate who has brought a gun to school (Garrett, 2001).
- 54 percent say it would be easy for them to get a gun (Langer, 1999).
- 67 percent say it would be easy for them to make a bomb (Langer, 1999).

Research has also shown that being bullied during middle school is predictive of low self-esteem 10 years later. By age 23, children who were bullied in middle school were more depressed and had lower self-esteem than their peers who had not been bullied. They feel more isolated than their peers, who often reject them out of fear that they, too, will become a target for bullies if they are seen with targeted students. This can lead to suicide or violent retaliation by victims.

By age 24, about 60 percent of the boys are identified as bullies in middle school had at least one conviction of a crime and 35 percent to 40 percent had three or more convictions. Half of all identified school bullies became criminals as adults. Furthermore, children who are bullies at age 8 are three times more likely to be convicted of a crime by age 30. Bullies are also less likely to finish college or locate a good job.

Bullying among primary age children has become recognized as an antecedent to more violent behavior in later years. Statistics on violence in our country tell a grim story with a clear message. Action is needed to end purposeful harassment and bullying.

Bullying in Middle Schools

As many as 80 percent of middle school students engage in bullying behaviors, say researchers, who also point to an increase in such incidents when children move from elementary to middle schools. Three different studies on bullying were presented at the American Psychology Association's 1999 Annual Conference, August 20–24 in Boston.

One study led by Dorothy Espelage and others from the University of Illinois found that many students tease their peers to go along with the crowd, but feel uncomfortable with their own behavior. Students who are physically different (race, body size, clothing) are more likely to be victimized, as are those who are good at things that everybody else is. And those who report bullying others often state they are bullied themselves.

Another study by Diana Paulk and others from the University of Nebraska-Lincoln questioned 83 sixth graders and six sixth grade teachers. They reported that about 75 percent of students had been bullies or victimized during the 1998–1999 school year. Students, more than teachers, overidentified other students as bullies or victims.

A third study by A.D. Pelligrini and others from the Universities of Minnesota and Georgia used a longitudinal approach. They assessed bullying attitudes of 154 fifth grade students, following up with them a year later when they entered middle school. Measurements included self-ratings on bullying behavior and victimization; ratings on their own and each other's popularity, friendships and feeling of isolation; teachers' ratings of the students' behavior; and other factors. Their findings supported that early adolescence witnesses an increase in aggression while youngsters look for new friendships. As soon as peer groups are formed, many of the aggressive behaviors subside.

The studies that have been done on the issue of bullying in this country and abroad have contributed to a growing body of knowledge that underscores the seriousness of the problem of bullying in the schools. The following is a list based on the current research about bullying:

- 80 percent of adolescents reported being bullied during their school years;
- 90 percent of 4th through 8th graders report being victims;
- 15 percent of students bully regularly or are victims of bullies;
- Up to 7 percent of 8th grade students stay home at least once a month because of bullies;
- Students reported that 71 percent of the teachers or other adults in the classroom ignored bullying incidents;
- When asked, students uniformly expressed the desire that teachers intervene rather than ignore teasing and bullying;
- Aggressive behavior is learned early and becomes resistant to change if it persists beyond age eight;
- Bullying often occurs in areas where there is minimal or no supervision (playgrounds, bathrooms, cafeteria);
- Most bullying is verbal;
- Both boys and girls bully, usually same sex classmates, with females using indirect, manipulative forms; and
- Bullying can have devastating long term effects on its victims.

National Institute of Child Health and Human Development Report

A report published in April 2001 by the National Institute of Child Health and Human Development, on the U.S. contribution to the

World Health Organization's Health Behavior in School-Age Children survey, found that 17 percent of the respondents bullied sometimes or weekly, 19 percent had bullied others sometimes or weekly, and 6 percent had both bullied others and been bullied (Bowman, 2001). The researchers estimated that 1.6 million children in grades 6 through 10 in the United States bully others as frequently. The survey, the first nationwide research on the problem in this country, questioned 15,686 public and private school students, grades 6 through 10, on their experiences with bullying. In a study of 6,500 middle school students in rural South Carolina, 23 percent said they had been bullied regularly during the previous 3 months and 20 percent admitted bullying another child regularly during that time.

Bullying behavior is a form of harassment and anti-social behavior which cross-cuts geographical, racial, and socioeconomic segments of society. It prevents students who are victims of bullying from enjoying a safe, stress-free learning environment. Students who are bullied report fear of going to school or riding the bus, physical symptoms of illness and progressively lower levels of self-esteem when continually faced with bullying behavior by their peers.

Studies on the Prevalence of Bullying

Toronto's Board of Education has documented that in grades 4 to 8, one child in five was victimized periodically, while one in 12 was bullied weekly or daily. Most bullying takes place in and around school and is often reinforced by an audience. In one study, 120 hours of video surveillance in Toronto schools showed that in over 20 percent of bullying, peers actively reinforced bullying by physically or verbally joining in the aggression. In 54 percent of cases, they reinforced the bully by watching but not joining in. In only 25 percent of cases did peers support the victim (Goldbloom, 2000).

A study led by Dr. Tonja Nansel and published in the *Journal of the American Medical Association* on April 25, 2001, surveyed 16,000 students throughout the United States. The study concluded that if you're a teenager today, you're one of the many who are on the giving or receiving end of bullying. The younger teens have it worse. Almost a third of teens are either bullies or are the victims. Nansel defines bullying as "when a teenager's behavior is purposely meant to harm or disturb another child, when it occurs over time, and when there is an imbalance of power between the kids involved." Types of bullying defined in the study included verbal belittling regarding religion, race, looks, or speech; hitting, pushing or slapping; spreading rumors; and making sexual comments or gestures. The study also found that both the perpetrators and the victims are lonelier than most kids and do not have very good relationships with their peers.

The Roots of Bullying

Researchers led by Kris Bosworth of the University of Arizona collected information from 558 students in grades 6 to 8 (Goldbloom, 2000). They divided the students into three groups: 228 who rarely or never bullied anyone; 243 who reported a moderate level of bullying; and 87 who reported excessive amounts of bullying. Those who reported the most bullying behavior had received more forceful, physical discipline from their parents, had viewed more television and showed more misconduct at home. Thirty-two percent lived with a step-parent, and 36 percent lived in a single-parent household. Bullies generally had fewer adult role models, more exposures to gang activity and easier access to guns. This partly explains why bullies need help as much as victims.

There are a lot of reasons why children bully. They may see it as a way of being popular, or making themselves look tough and in charge. Some bullies do it to get attention or to make others afraid of them. Others may be jealous of the person they are bullying. They may be being bullied themselves. Some bullies may not even understand how wrong their behavior is and how it makes the person being bullied feel.

Maine Research

The Maine Project Against Bullying (MPAB) established baseline data on bullying in that state by surveying third graders in 1999. The survey was funded through the Maine Department of Education through a Carl D. Perkins grant, in collaboration with the Muskie Institute and the University of Southern Maine. An analysis of the data collected revealed that 22.6 percent of third graders surveyed said they were threatened, 40.7 percent were teased in a mean way, 40 percent were called hurtful names, 34.3 percent were left out of things on purpose, and 37.5 percent were hit, kicked, or pushed every day, once or twice a week, or once or twice month. Of surveyed students confronted with bullying, 91.3 percent report taking action in response. Most children (44.6 percent) told an adult, 34.2 percent told the bully to stop, 32 percent got away from the bully. Students reported that when they told someone about the bullying, 48.2 percent said it got better, while 15 percent said it got worse and 21.7 percent said nothing happened. It should be noted that 5.9 percent never told anyone. It is consistently reported in the research that victims sometimes do not report bullying for fear of retaliation from the bully.

There is a difference between genders when children participating in the survey blamed the perpetrator. A higher percentage of boys (30.1 percent) than girls (18.9 percent) reported being bullied by a boy, while a higher percentage of girls (13.2 percent) than boys (4.8 percent) reported being bullied by a girl. Similarly, a higher percentage of boys (24.7 percent) than girls (15.0 percent) reported a boy tried to hurt them, while a higher percentage of girls (5.9 percent) than boys (3.25) reported a girl tried to hurt them. Generally speaking, when children reported about those responsible for milder as well as more serious bullying acts, they often said (40.6 percent) that a boy had committed the offense.

These Maine survey results show that for 37 percent of victims who seek help against a bully, the situation continues as it is, or worsens. This perceived lack of assistance at school for victimized students gives the implicit message that these behaviors are acceptable.

Of the third graders surveyed, 13.8 to 17.7 percent reported they participated in the identified bullying behaviors every day, or once or twice a week or month. Olweus (1993a) found that there was a stability of bully-victim problems over time. Children who bully and children who are victimized tend to perpetuate these roles throughout their school years. Educators must help these students as early as possible in their school careers in order to have a chance of changing these emerging, harmful patterns of behavior.

Research indicates, and the Maine Project supports, that bullying behavior is an antecedent of more serious harassing and antisocial behavior. Bullying and harassment are community issues that need a multifaceted, systematic approach that includes all community stakeholders.

New Zealand Study

Dr. Gabrielle Maxwell and Janis Carroll-Lind (1977) conducted research in New Zealand on bullying. The research was aimed at examining the child's perspective on what is violent for them and the impact these violent events have on their lives. The study involved violence at home, the community and the school. A total of 259 children took part with an even mix of boys and girls spreading across the immediate age range of 11 to 13 years. The study confirms high levels of both physical and emotional bullying in New Zealand schools. Within any particular year, it is likely that at least half and perhaps as many as three quarters of children are bullied. Ten percent are bullied weekly.

Why Is Bullying Harmful?

Bullying may seem like a normal part of a child's world and a way they learn to stand up for themselves. But it makes many children feel lonely, unhappy, frightened and unsafe. Some victims blame themselves because they think there must be something wrong with them. Signs that might indicate a child is being bullied include:

- Stomach aches
- Nightmares
- Reluctance to go to school
- Loss of confidence
- Loss of contact with friends
- Isolation

Why Are Children Bullied?

Some children are bullied for no particular reason, but normally it's because they are different — perhaps it's the color of their skin, the way they talk, their size or their name. Sometimes children are bullied because they look like they won't stand up for themselves — they are viewed as lacking confidence to take action. Playground observation research has shown that one incident of bullying occurs every seven minutes.

Adult intervention occurs in 4 percent of incidents, and peers intervene in 11 percent of incidents. No interventions take place in 85 percent of incidents. What conclusions can bullies draw from this? What conclusions can victims draw from this?

There are numerous risk factors to be addressed if we are going to eliminate the causes of bullying. Family behavior, the child's personality, the school climate and community climate can contribute to bullying.

Family Factors

The home is the most violent place in the United States (Straus, 1994). And contrary to popular belief, the majority of violence directed at young children in the home comes from the mother and older siblings (Straus and Gelles, 1988). Weinhold and Weinhold (2000) outline three primary predictive family factors:

- A lack of solid bonding or attachment with the young child.
- Poor supervision and neglect of the child's needs.
- Acceptance and modeling of aggressive or bullying behaviors by parents or older siblings.

Personality Factors

Some personality characteristics are common among bullies:
- Children with an impulsive temperament are more inclined to develop into a bully (Olweus, 1994).
- Boys who are physically bigger or stronger than peers of the same age are more likely to become bullies (Olweus, 1993).
- Bullies like to be in charge, dominate, and assert their power. They like to win at all costs (Olweus, 1993).
- Bullies crave attention, so they show off and act tough in order to get it from their peers (Olweus, 1994).
- Bullies lack empathy for their victims and have difficulty feeling compassion (Olweus, 1993).
- Bullies believe the victim provoked the attack and deserves the consequences (Olweus, 1994).
- Bullying is a cry for help (Olweus, 1994).

School Factors

The response of adults, or lack of it, plays a key role in creating a school climate that tolerates or discourages bullying. Researchers have found:
- The amount of adult supervision is directly tied to the frequency and severity of bullying in schools (Saunders, 1997).
- A negative school climate where negative behavior gets most of the attention encourages the formation of cliques and bullying (Espelage et al., 1999).
- Some teachers threaten, tease or intimidate students to maintain control of their classroom (Olweus, 1994).
- 25 percent of the teachers see nothing wrong with bullying and put-downs. Schools condone this behavior and do nothing to prevent bullying and put-downs (Olweus, 1994).
- The learning environment can be poisoned by bullying and put-downs, raising the fear and anxiety of all students (Johnson and Johnson, 1995).
- Identification and early intervention programs are lacking in many schools. Bullies can be identified as early as pre-school (Olweus, 1994).

Community Factors

Hawkins and Catalano et al. (1992), identify characteristics of communities that may contribute to bullying behavior on the part of children. They have found:
- Schools in poor urban neighborhoods experience more violence in and around the schools.
- People feel less safe in neighborhoods where there is evidence of crack houses and drug dealing–related violence. This spills over into the neighborhood schools, where there is more drug dealing–related violence.
- Schools located in neighborhoods with high turnover also have more bullying.
- State and local policies on early identification and intervention can influence a community's intolerance to such behavior.

How Does Bullying Differ from Normal Peer Conflicts?

There is a big difference between bullying and normal peer conflicts (Weinhold, 1999). In a bullying situation, there are several defining factors:

- Intent to harm. The perpetrator finds pleasure in taunting or trying to dominate the victim and continues even when the victim's distress is obvious.
- Intensity and duration. The bullying continues over a long period of time and the degree of bullying is damaging to the self-esteem of the victim.
- Power of the bully. The bully has power over the victim because of age, strength, size or gender.
- Vulnerability of the victim. The victim is more sensitive to the teasing, cannot adequately defend him or herself, and has physical or psychological qualities that make him or her more prone to victimization.
- Lack of support. The victim feels isolated and exposed. Often, the victim is afraid to report the bullying for fear of retaliation.
- Consequences. The damage to the victim's self-esteem is long lasting and leads the victim to markedly withdraw from school, or they too become aggressive.

In a normal peer conflict situation, none of these elements are present, so those who are involved in a normal peer conflict:

- Do not insist on getting their own way.
- Give reasons why they disagree.
- Apologize or offer win-win suggestions.
- Are free to bargain and negotiate to get their needs met.
- Can change the topic and walk away.

Profile of a Bully

The following are fictitious profiles of children who are at risk of becoming a bully.

PROFILE: SAM, 10 YEARS OLD

School: Sam lives in a middle class neighborhood with one of his biological parents. He is always telling jokes and funny stories. He is very large for his age in both height and weight. He tries to hang around with the older boys both before and after school. Other children describe him as being mean. He always tries to act cool. Sam can be very hot tempered in a confrontational situation. He is very prejudiced and is constantly calling others nigger or yeller.

Domestic: He has a love-hate relationship with his mother; he never talks about his father. He hates his younger sister and is constantly hitting her, pushing her and calling her names. He erupts violently with no apparent reason and retreats to his room. He does not allow his mother or sister to enter his room.

PROFILE: JOE, 12 YEARS OLD

School: Joe constantly picks on younger, smaller children; this is especially evident as he walks to school. He is average in size and participates in team sports. He talks back to his teachers and does not show respect to the principal. He takes lunch money from the third graders frequently. He tells certain sixth grade students they are "weird," "fat," "too short," or "your smile looks like your teeth fell out." Other outbursts include telling other students they are stupid, geeky, or dumb.

Domestic: Joe lives with his father and stepbrother. There is no female figure in the household. His father works double shifts and is never at home. He is responsible for the after school care of his five year old stepbrother. Joe is constantly mistreating his stepbrother and often threatens him with bodily harm. Joe spends a lot of time strolling the neighborhood and hanging with high school kids. He is experimenting with cigarettes and alcohol. Also, he just got a computer and has become involved in several chat rooms pertaining to "Skin Heads."

PROFILE: MIKE, 7 YEARS OLD

School: Has not mastered reading and has difficulty writing. He is constantly being called down by the teacher because he does not listen. He is very large for his age and has difficulty relating to his peers. The other boys and girls are afraid of him because of his temper. However, when they are allowed to select their peers to be on their team during physical education, Mike is always selected first.

Domestic: Mike lives in a household with seven brothers and sisters. He is the middle child and is constantly seeking attention. His older brothers are constantly beating him up but he never tells his parents. Frequently, he will kick the dog or throw the cat down the stairs. Both parents work and they do not share their meals together.

PROFILE: BOB, 13 YEARS OLD

School: Bob is not passing any of his core or encore courses except physical education. He has been retained once for not performing on grade level and spends a lot of time in the principal's office for fighting, cursing or other inappropriate behavior. He thinks it's not really his fault; the principal and the teachers don't like him — they never have. His latest school incident was beating up a sixth grade child while waiting for the bus. Bob's father had to come to school and told the principal that Bob had to protect himself. Even though Bob beat up a sixth grade child who was much smaller than him, it was still okay because the other kid was running his mouth at Bob.

Domestic: Lives on the wrong side of town. Comes home daily to an empty house. His mother abandoned him when he was eight years old. His father is an alcoholic and often tells Bob if he doesn't take up for himself, he will beat him. When his dad drinks he is often in a rage and has been jailed himself for assault and disturbing the peace. Meals are normally fast food or from cans or boxes; whatever Bob can get. Bob qualifies for free lunch at school but his dad won't let him accept it.

PROFILE: TERRI, 16 YEARS OLD

School: Terri is the kind of girl who always gets her way, no matter what. She'll do anything to get what she wants and doesn't care what others think of her. She usually hangs around with some other tough girls and most of the kids in school have learned not to cross her. Every day for the last two weeks Terri has been extorting lunch money from Sandy, a younger girl. When Sandy enters the cafeteria, Terri or one of her gang approaches her, demanding a favored snack from her lunch or money. Terri threatens that if Sandy doesn't give in, her hair will be cut, her clothes torn, and she'll be beaten up. Sandy's mother phones the school after battling with her daughter every day to go to school. In the last month Sandy has missed at least two days a week of school because she complaints of dizziness and an upset stomach.

Domestic: Terri comes from a middle class family — both parents are professionals. There is a total of five children in the family and Terri is the middle child. Due to both parents working, there is very little adult supervision in the mornings and afternoons. When both parents are home there is a lot of screaming between the parents. The dad has physically abused the mother on several occasions.

Profile of a Victim

The following are fictitious profiles of children or adults who are at risk or have been victimized:

PROFILE: JOEY, 11 YEARS OLD

Joey dreads going to school each day. Several boys in his class turned against him weeks ago. They whisper behind his back, ignore him when he talks, move away from him when he sits down, leave nasty letters for him and exclude him from school activities. Joey has tried talking to them to work things out, but that hasn't worked. He wonders if he's wearing the wrong type of clothes or behaving the wrong way. The more he tries to fit in, the worse the bullying seems to get. He is afraid to tell his teachers or parents — they might say that he's being silly or exaggerating, and should try to solve his own problems. If he tells, the guys will get mad and be even meaner.

PROFILE: THOMASINE, 8 YEARS OLD

Thomasine is in fourth grade and is having trouble concentrating in school — her grade point average is dropping from A's to C's and maybe a D in reading. Julie is the real problem. She started teasing Thomasine last year and hasn't stopped since. Now Thomasine tries to stay inside the classroom during recess. When she goes out, Julie is always on the lookout for her — and for any teachers who might be watching. Julie roughs her up — Thomasine tries not to cry as her hair is being pulled and her dress is torn. Sometimes the other classmates join in, kicking and pushing and calling her names. Thomasine's teacher doesn't know about this but she has told her parents about the bullying. They are really worried and want to tell the principal but Thomasine begs them not to do this. She's been told by Julie that if she ever tells, she will be in big trouble.

PROFILE: GARY, 14 YEARS OLD

Gary is an eight grade honors student who went to the doctor for treatment of asthma and for an assessment of acne. When Gary first visited the doctor he was of average height and weight and looked like a normal, healthy teenager. Two months after Gary's initial visit to the doctor, he went back to the doctor for a checkup. Gary had lost ten pounds, the acne had not improved and he was having difficulty in school. He indicated that he did not like attending school because he was constantly being teased and bullied. During the conversation with the doctor, Gary cried. He had always been shy and without many friends but he had never been a target for bullying. He did not know what was happening in eighth grade and he did not know how to deal with it. His parents tried to intervene at school by asking if he could change classrooms, but this request was denied. Now, everyone was just waiting for the school year to end, hoping that the next school year would be better. Gary was not sleeping well. He voiced serious depression. He was not going out after school, his interest and academic effort were declining, and he wanted to be home-schooled.

PROFILE: BILL, ADULT

Bill recalls, "When I was a young boy, the bully called me names, stole my notebooks, forced me off the playground. He made fun of me in from of other children, forced me to give him my lunch money each day, and threatened to beat me up if I told the teacher. At different times I was subject to a wide variety of degradation and abuse — spitting in my face, making me eat dirt, and breaking my glasses. To this day ... I remember every detail."

PROFILE: JOHN, ADULT

"My bully lived across the street from me. He'd taunt me and tease me. I was very sensitive, small for my age and I spent my free time playing the piano and reading. I didn't participate in sports and I was shy with people I didn't know. David, the bully, knew I was vulnerable and took great delight in threatening me. I don't recall him actually hitting me but I was very uncomfortable when I saw him outside his house because I knew I had been selected for his verbal abuse. The fact that I remember the experience thirty years later proves how humiliating and degrading bullying can be to a victim."

PROFILE: MARK, ADULT
"I'm an adult now, 67 years old. I can recall to this very day, Bricker, the football player at Joy High School, he made a practice of bullying me each and every day. The memories are fresh although they happened almost 52 years ago. Each day he called me four-eyes and punched me in the stomach. I always tried to avoid him in the hallways but he always found me. In the gym he constantly hit me with wet towels and one time he hid my pants. Other times he put chewing gum in my hair and slammed the locker on my hands. I will never forget these painful experiences."

Bullying Behaviors

When identifying children who have tendencies to bully, we can never be sure how accurate they are or that we are stereotyping. No one symptom stands out to imply a bullying behavior. As parents, educators, and community members, we must observe our children for certain traits. In this way we can establish a pattern of mild, moderate or severe levels of potential bullying.

In most cases, there are early warning signs that children who have bullying tendencies will harm themselves or others—certain behavioral and emotional signs that, when viewed in context, can tell us we have a troubled child. However, early warnings are just that—indicators that a child may need help.

Such signs may or may not indicate a serious problem. When a profile was presented to school principals, their response was: how many characteristics does a child display before I seek action? Early warning signs provide us with the impetus to check out our concerns and address the child's needs; they allow us to act responsibly by getting help for the child before problems escalate.

It's important to avoid inappropriately labeling or stigmatizing individual students because they appear to fit a specific profile or set of early warning indicators. Teachers and administrators—and other school staff—are not professionally trained to analyze children's feelings, motives and behaviors. However, they see these children every day, eight hours a day. Effective schools offer special training to identify children who are bullies and may have violent tendencies.

Educators, families and communities can increase their ability to recognize early warning signs by establishing close, caring and supportive relationships with children and youth. Unfortunately, however, there is a real danger that early warning signs can be misinterpreted. Nonetheless, certain behaviors and characteristics should alert educators to the possibility that a child is bullying others. These may include the following.

Verbal Abuse (General Name Calling)

- Using accusatory terms such as fag, gay, lesbian, or shrew.
- Calling other people names just to be mean ... geek, four-eyes, shrimp, wimp, fruitcake.
- Giving other children dirty looks.
- Making fun of their religion or nationality by calling them names like Jew Boy, Wop, Spick, Yellow, or Jap.
- Telling others they are no good: "You can't do this, nobody likes you, get away."
- Calling others crazy.
- Abusing their parents or family members: "Your mother is poor as dirt," "Your brother's dumb as a door nail," or "Your whole family is crazy."

Verbal Abuse (Appearance)

- Making fun of a child's appearance by using terms like metal face, metal mouth or midget.
- Using put-downs like "You're skinny as a rail," "Your smile looks like your teeth fell out," "You're ugly," or "You're fat," or "You're too tall."
- Questioning another child's care: "Don't you have anything else to wear?" or "You stink — don't you take showers?"

Verbal Abuse (Academics)

- Assailing another child's academic abilities by calling them retarded, teacher's pet, and the like.
- Making another child feel inadequate by saying things like, "You sure got the short end of the stick when they gave out brains, "Don't you have any common sense?" "You're stupid because you can't read," or "You're dumb because you can't do that math problem."
- Belittling another's successes with phrases like, "Don't you have a life after school?" or "He's a geek, he knows more than the teacher."

Verbal Abuse (Athletics)

- "Can't you run any faster?"
- "You are so weak."
- "What a wimp!"
- "You kick like your momma."
- "You can't do anything right."
- "What? You got two left feet?"
- "You are so slow you wouldn't be able to catch the lice."
- "Our team won — because we're the best. Your team stinks."

Spreading Rumors

- Talking behind other people's backs and starting rumors
- Telling someone a secret that really is not the truth. Then the next person tells someone else and the entire thought is miscommunicated.
- Passing notes which contain cruel statements about others.
- Telling lies on others that are demeaning and hurtful.

Prejudice

- Calling other names like white trash, black trash, or Mexican trash.
- Putting down another's religion. If they don't believe in something you believe in, they think yours is a dumb belief.

Physically Hurting

- Beating up on smaller and or younger children.
- Punching others until they start to cry.
- Pushing and shoving others or elbowing.
- Fighting with others in front of the victim's friends or girlfriend.
- Throwing things at or on them — such as milk or food in the cafeteria.

Pranks and Mean Games

- Making others drop their books or papers.
- Tripping others and laughing when they fall.
- Emptying another person's book bag in front of others.
- Hitting others as they are standing in line.
- Cutting in line and cutting others off when they are talking.
- Picking smaller kids up and making them into flying airplanes.
- Stuffing others into a trashcan or dumpster.

Destroying Property

- Taking lunch money from others.
- Spitting on an individual's clothing or possessions.
- Cutting someone's hair (this can also be considered assault).
- Destroying others' property such as throwing paint on someone's jacket or cutting holes in someone's gym shorts.

Personality Characteristics

- Mean.
- Arrogant.
- Always putting other kids down — very degrading.
- Acting like they're better than everyone else.
- Acting like they can do anything they want because they're older or bigger than everyone else.
- Always having to be the best or the center of attention.

Poor Emotional Self-Control

- Having a lot of hatred or built-up frustrations.

- Hot tempered — very excitable.
- Rude, always in your face.

Crowd Pleaser

- Always the class clown.
- Always going with what their friends say — not what their heart tells them.
Physical characteristics
- Average size or the largest one in the class.
- Possibly athletic and think they're better than the others.
- Wearing baggy pants or shorts—cool clothes, especially boys.
- Wearing very fashionable hair styles.

Poor Support System

- Treated poorly at home, bullies often witness the violent behavior of parents or relatives. (Children from violent homes are three or four times more likely to become a bully.)
- Parents lack a solid bonding or attachment with the young child.
- There is poor supervision and neglect of the child's needs.
- There is acceptance and modeling of aggressive or bullying behaviors by parents or older siblings.

Isolation

- Bullies don't have a lot of close friends.
- They are envious of fellow classmates.
- They may not be very popular and use bullying as a way of getting attention.

Behavioral Characteristics

- Getting in trouble at school either with the principal or teacher.
- Showing a lack of respect for authority or resisting authoritative figures.
- Talking back to adults.
- Performing poorly in academic areas.

Attitudes and Feelings

- They are bossy.
- They are nice to others outside of class or when others are not around.
- They interrupt when others are speaking.
- They laugh when something is really not funny but is demeaning.

—————— *Perspectives on Bullying* ——————

When tenth grade students at an alternative high school (Clyde, N.C.) were asked what bullying meant to them, they replied:
- Making fun of someone,
- Insulting others,
- Cussing others,
- Calling people names or calling family members names,
- Picking on others,
- Teasing when it's not funny,
- Spreading rumors about others—just being mean and nasty to someone,
- Being jealous of someone and saying nasty things about them,
- Pushing, shoving, fighting,
- Picking on kids that are smaller than you,
- Bossing others— making them your servant,
- Treating another human being the way you would not want to be treated,
- Taking stuff from others— school supplies, lunch money or clothes,
- Name calling,
- Taunting others,
- Making fun of people,
- Staring at people in a mean way, and
- Playing mind games—spreading rumors.

These students also said bullying is a problem after school or when teachers are not around, and that it happens every day either at school or in their community. Freshmen, particularly are the victims of bullies in high school, especially if they're small and smart. While every school can expect to have a bully, and it can happen anywhere, these students felt bullying was not a big problem at their school because everyone gets along.

Students attending summer schools in North Carolina were asked to talk about bullying in their schools. The results are as follows:

Seventh Grade Boy : "Our school is really large and sometimes when I'm by myself I get scared. A lot of people get picked on or bullied and you can't really do nothing about it. Most of the kids won't tell the principal because they're afraid of being called a tattle-tale. If you tell the principal it will just make it worse."

Eleventh Grade Boy: "When I went to middle school, I was a short, fat kid. My hair was cut in a bowl shape and my voice sounded weird. I was called 'faggot' a lot because I was in the drama club. I thought every kid went through this. But when I got to high school I had changed, I wasn't fat, I was average height and my voice was ok. I think there's a tendency to disregard bullying as a natural part of childhood."

Tenth Grade Girl: "Bullying is not something you actually see as you walk the school hallways. It's an under current — it happens beneath the surface. People who get bullied don't necessarily talk about it. I think the school does its best to protect students but they can be everywhere all day long."

Ninth Grade Girl: "Most of the teachers are in the hallways. If there's a fight they always break it up. That's all they really do."

Eleventh Grade Girl: "Security at my school is very tight. There's a school resource officer and we have a male principal and assistant principal. We really don't have any problems; our principal would expel them."

Tenth Grade Boy: "I think students need to play a more active role in defending other students. Students just walk by and let things happen. Most of the bullying I see is groups of people picking on one another. If people stepped in it might make the people who are picking on this one person stop."

Sixth Grade Boy: "You can't stop a student from what they want to do. And if they want to do something, they'll do it. Nowhere is safe, honestly. We write bills that nobody listens to; we make rules nobody follows, we make changes where nobody wants to participate. You have to make people want to change. What I don't understand is why don't people tell an adult when someone is bullying them."

——— *An Old Problem Reconsidered* ———

Six million boys and four million girls are involved in fights every year on school grounds. Many are physically threatened while a large number of students are robbed.

Bullying has become a very hot and controversial issue. It's been in the news, and the theme of several talk shows in the past year. The problem has been around for as long as we've had schools. But it's only recently that we've become aware enough to do something about it.

Children between the ages of 5 and 11 begin using verbal abuse and are capable of some physical abuse such as fist fighting, kicking and choking. However, once a child reaches the age of 12, psychological changes take place and the bullying becomes more violent. This might include the use of weapons and sexual abuse.

Murder among children was up 35 percent in 1997. Today's 3, 4 and 5 year olds could grow up to be a generation of serial killers. Some signs to watch for in younger children include setting fires and torturing animals (Garrett, 2001).

Chapter Two, Myths and Truths About Bullying, will focus on how bullies are really raised in the home, but their victims are too frequently created in the classroom. Myths about bullies and the research that helped identify those myths will be stressed. Because of these myths, many of the ways we have dealt with bullies and their victims have often made the problem worse.

TWO

Myths and Truths About Bullying

How prevalent is bullying? One in seven children is a bully or the target of a bully, according to the National Association of School Psychologists. Targets of teasing and bullying often remain silent, but they may suffer the effects, such as lack of self-confidence, underachievement in school and withdrawal.

While school crime is decreasing, students feel less safe at school. This climate of fear erodes the quality of education and learning.

If teachers and parents are to successfully prevent or eliminate bullying in their classrooms, they need to understand the characteristics of bullies and their victims. According to leading experts, much of what we have always believed about bullying is wrong, and consequently many of our techniques for dealing with bullies and their victims have simply made the problem worse. Bullies are not, the research indicates, cowardly misfits with low self-esteem. Some fit this description, but the majority do not. Their victims are rarely chosen because of the color of their hair or skin or the shape of their glasses. Most importantly, bullying is not a problem that will go away without adult intervention.

Presented in this chapter are numerous myths and facts concerning bullies and their victims. Research will be presented for each myth.

Myth: Bullying is not a problem in the schools.

Fact: Every day in our nation's schools, children are threatened, teased, taunted and tormented by schoolyard bullies. For some children, bullying is a fact of life that they are to accept as part of growing up. Those who fail to recognize and stop bullying practices as they

34

occur actually promote violence, sending the message to children that bullying is okay.

Bullies were once considered to be an inevitable part of school life; however, the experience of being picked on, teased, or regularly harassed has never been a pleasant experience. Few childhood memories are as powerful as those of the class bully and his or her unfortunate victims.

Bullying often leads to greater and prolonged violence in the schools. Not only does it harm its intended victims, but it also negatively affects the climate of schools and the opportunities for all children to learn and achieve.

Bullying among school children is quite common in the United States. In a study of junior high and high school students from small Midwestern towns, 88 percent of students said they had observed bullying, and 76.8 percent indicated they had been a victim of bullying at school. Of the nearly 77 percent who had been victimized, 14 percent indicated they had experienced severe reactions to the abuse (Bitney, 2001).

A study of 6,500 fourth to sixth graders in rural South Carolina indicated that during the three months preceding the study, one in four students had been bullied with some regularity and one in 10 had been bullied at least once a week. In the same survey, approximately one in five children admitted they had been bullied with some regularity during the three months preceding the study (Bitney, 2001).

Various reports and studies have established that approximately 15 percent of students are either bullied regularly or are initiators of bullying behavior (Olweus, 1993).

Direct bullying seems to increase through the elementary years, peak in the middle or junior high years, and decline during high school. However, while direct physical assault seems to decrease with age, verbal abuse appears to remain constant. School size, racial composition, and school setting (rural, suburban, or urban) do not seem to be distinguishing factors in predicting the occurrence of bullying.

One half of all violence against teenagers occurs in school buildings, on school property or on the street in the vicinity of the school (NIDR, 1999).

The National School Safety Center estimates there are over 525,000 attacks, shakedowns and robberies per month in public secondary schools in this country (Weinhold and Weinhold, 1998).

The National Educators Association estimates that 160,000 students miss school every day, totaling 28 million missed days per year, due to fear of attack or intimidation by a bully. Students receive an average of 213 verbal put-downs per week, or 30 per day (Fried and Fried, 1996).

Ninety percent of all students felt that bullying caused social, emotional, or academic problems for those students who were bullied. Sixty percent of all students believe that schools respond poorly to bullying and victimization (Weinhold and Weinhold, 2000).

Bullying occurs in every school and in every grade throughout the world. There are no exceptions and anyone who thinks otherwise is being extremely unrealistic and naive.

It's in the schools which say "there's no bullying here" that you are most likely to find it. Good schools are proactive and deal with it promptly, firmly and fairly. Bad schools deny it, ignore it, rationalize it, handle it inappropriately, sweep it under the carpet, blame the victim of bullying, blame the parents of the victim of bullying, or make lots of impressive noises but take no substantive action.

In Washington, D.C., four out of five students—boys and girls—reported they have experienced some type of sexual harassment in school, despite a greater awareness of school policies dealing with the issue. Harassing words and actions happen often, occur under teachers' noses, can begin in elementary school, and are very upsetting to both boys and girls (Olweus and Limber, 1999).

There are approximately 2.1 million bullies and 2.7 million of their targets in our schools (Olweus, National School Safety Center).

United States Secretary of Education Rod Paige (August, 2002) reacted to reports of harassment of Muslim and Arab American students by asking teachers to discuss diversity and tolerance with their students. He has called on educators to prevent harassment and bullying by encouraging students to discuss the diversity constructively and express ideological differences respectfully.

The North Dakota Department of Public Instruction conducted a study in 1999 to determine the nature of safety and violence in the school setting. They interviewed parents, students, and educators by telephone and questionnaire. The study concluded with these findings:

- Bullying and verbal abuse are the behaviors with which parents and principals are most concerned.

- Thirty percent of the responding principals said violence/aggressive behavior in general was getting worse at their school.
- There is a need for focused training activities related to specific behaviors such as bullying. Only 53 percent of the schools provide this service to staff, and only 11.5 percent to parents.

Once considered sanctuaries of innocence and learning, American schools today are often perceived as dangerous places. The public recently has been inundated by images of children shooting classmates and teachers, leading to fears that violence is becoming a horrifying trend in our schools across the nation. Bullying seems to be one of the major culprits of violence. Bullying includes intentional exclusion, intimidation, persistent teasing, poking, hitting, or extorting money, food or toys from another child. This behavior commonly occurs when there is little adult supervision.

According to research done by Janice Gallagher, one of four children is bullied, and one out of five defines themselves as a bully. Approximately 282,000 students are physically attacked in secondary schools every month (Vail, 1999).

Many children avoid public areas of the school such as the cafeteria and restrooms in an attempt to elude bullies. For some students, the fear is so great that they avoid school altogether. Every day approximately 160,000 students stay home from school because they are afraid of being bullied (Vail, 1999).

"The problem of bullying is in all schools," says Wendy Craig (1995), professor of psychology at Queens University in Kingston, Ontario. "If schools don't acknowledge it they inadvertently support it. If schools don't address the problem, we know it will get worse. It's like an infection — if you don't take steps early to stop it, it will grow."

Myth: Children from good homes are not bullies.

Fact: Usually bullies come from middle-class families that do not monitor their children's activities. The parents of bullies are either extremely tolerant and permissive, and allow them to get away with everything, or they are physically aggressive and abusive.

Bullies often come from homes where physical punishment is used, where the children are taught to strike back physically as a way to handle problems, and where parental involvement and warmth are frequently lacking. However, this is not always the case.

Too frequently bullies come from homes where bullying occurs among adults and family members. In this situation, children are imitating their role models. A number of child-rearing styles have been found to predict whether children will grow up to become bullies. A lack of attention and warmth toward the child, together with modeling of aggressive behavior at home and poor supervision of the child, provide the perfect opportunity for aggressive and bullying behavior to occur. Modeling may include use of physical and verbal aggression toward the child by parents, or use of physical and verbal aggression by parents toward each other. The connection between children witnessing wife assault then engaging in bullying behavior toward peers has not been well studied, but studies do indicate that aggressive behavior of all kinds is elevated in children who witness violence by their father toward their mother (Jaffe, Wolfe and Wilson, 1990).

Supervision of children has been found to be of prime importance. Low levels of supervision in the home are associated with the development of bully problems in individual children.

Myth: Ignore bullies and they will stop.

Fact: Never ignore bullying: bullies use provocation to get a response out of their target and if you ignore it the provocation will get worse. When people ignore something it means they don't engage and don't respond. When bullying begins, students should recognize it immediately, keep a log of events and get parents and teachers involved. They have a right not to be bullied, harassed, assaulted or abused.

The American Medical Association recognizes that bullying is a public health problem. Abuse of children by other children may contribute to violent behavior, addiction, criminal activity and other ills of society. Public health advocates are increasingly recognizing that the death toll from the violent incidents that have swept the nation are just the tip of the iceberg in terms of negative implications—both for bullies and their victims. Bullying is being looked at as a factor in many of society's ills, including smoking, underage drinking, mental illness and drug addiction. It's also seen as the root of more violent behavior, particularly among adults. Since the Columbine massacre, several medical organizations have increased the attention paid to bullying. Most recently, the American Medical Association announced it would address bullying as part of its anti-violence campaign. The Association also will support research on the subject and prepare materials that will help people and institutions deal with the issue. Part of the challenge, though, is to overcome the common view that bullying is a normal part of childhood and adolescence.

Myth: Bullies are just immature — they wouldn't harm anyone.

Fact: Bullying and the harm that it causes are seriously underestimated by many children and adults. Educators, parents, and children concerned with violence prevention must also be concerned with the phenomenon of bullying and its link to other violent behaviors.

Bullycide is a term used to describe when children choose suicide rather than face another day of unrelenting bullying.

- At least 16 children commit bullycide in the UK every year.
- 19,999 children attempt suicide annually — one every half hour
- About 2 million children see their physician each year for emotional and psychological problems (Marr and Field).

At Columbine High's feeder elementary schools, where the innocence of young children still reigns, the fears have been quicker to subside, and the path to status quo a little smoother. Crisis plans have been formed by each school which include how to deal with hostage situations, explosives and any kind of violent acts. In day to day teaching, they have developed zero tolerance for teasing or taunting. The schools have also developed a peer mediation program to teach students to resolve conflicts.

Tizon (1996) offers this example:

> Two years ago Barry Loukaitis, a junior high student in Mosed Lake, Washington, walked into an algebra class carrying a rifle under a trench coat. He pointed the gun at a student sitting next to the door and pulled the trigger. The boy died instantly. During the next fifteen minutes he shot two more classmates and his teacher. Only one victim survived the attack. The first student he killed, Manuel Vela, Jr., was popular, athletic and often bullied him. Loukaitis's name was listed on the honor roll before he brought national attention to his small town. His classmates described him as a shy and serious loner, someone with few friends who was a much-used target for harassment. According to students his large feet, his gangly build, his studiousness and his cowboy clothing were attributes that made him an easy candidate for bullying.

As established by studies in Scandinavian countries, a strong correlation appears to exist between bullying other students during the school years and experiencing legal or criminal troubles as adults. In one study, 60 percent of those characterized as bullies in grades six through nine had at least one criminal conviction by age 24 (Olweus,

1993). Chronic bullies seem to maintain their behaviors into adulthood, negatively influencing their ability to develop and maintain positive relationships (Oliver, Hoover and Hazler, 1994).

At one time, bullying was viewed as harmless, but many researchers agree that decreasing social violence lies in the prevention of bullying behavior (Fried and Fried, 1996). Researchers are also discovering repercussions to being bullied, ranging from an interference with the victim's learning to depression, which in extreme cases can lead to suicide. An estimated half a million students are marked absent every 30 days because of bullying nationwide (Sampson, 2000). And 10 percent of high school dropouts left school because of bullying. Bullies themselves are at risk for serious antisocial and criminal behavior in adulthood.

Finland researchers conducted a study to investigate the association between bullying, depression and suicide among adolescents aged 14 to 16. It was concluded that children who were bullied frequently at school were more likely to wet their beds, have difficulty sleeping, and have headaches and abdominal pain. There is a correlation between those bullied and anxiety, a fear of going to school, feeling unsafe at school and being unhappy. Depression has been linked with being bullied. The possible association between being bullied and the risk of suicide has been recognized by psychiatrists specializing in adolescence. Being a bully in childhood and adolescence has been associated with delinquency in adulthood. Being bullied has been associated with poorer perceived health, depression, and mental disorders in adulthood.

Myth: Boys are the only bullies.

Fact: While boys typically engage in direct bullying methods, girls who bully are more apt to utilize more subtle, indirect strategies, such as spreading rumors and enforcing social isolation (Ahmad and Smith, 1994). Whether the bullying is direct or indirect, the key component of bullying is that the physical or psychological intimidation occurs repeatedly over time to create an ongoing pattern of harassment and abuse. Boys engage in bullying behavior and are victims of bullies more frequently than girls (Batsche and Knoff, 1994).

Boys bully both boys and girls, while girls tend to bully other girls. Victims are usually taunted because of their physical appearance. Boys may be singled out based on their small size or perceived weakness, and girls who mature early are prone to teasing, which may later lead to harassment.

Many boys who have been bullies continue their style of behavior in later life. As adults they are at increased risk for criminality, marital violence, child abuse and sexual harassment. Beginning in 1961, Drs. Donald West and David Farrington of Cambridge University studied boys ages 8 to 32. They found convicted delinquents had previously tended to be troublesome and dishonest in their primary schools, only to become aggressive and frequent liars at age 12 to 14 and bullies at age 14.

Males in our country are about nine times as homicidal as females. Male aggression cannot be entirely explained sociologically. In most animal species, males are more aggressive because androgens affect brain structure and function. But most boys and most men are not violent. Unfortunately, mental illness and neurological impairment in boys and men are likely to be manifested in aggressive behavior.

Myth: Most bullying occurs off school grounds.

Fact: Although some bullying occurs outside the school or on the way to and from school, most occurs on school grounds: in classrooms, in hallways and on playgrounds. Bullying is a part of the overall culture of violence that is supported by dominator values, and it occurs everywhere.

Myth: Bullies are just normal people.

Fact: Some bullies are outgoing, aggressive, active and expressive. They get their way by brute force or openly harassing someone. This type of bully rejects rules and regulations and needs to rebel to achieve a feeling of superiority and security. Other bullies are more reserved and manipulative and may not want to be recognized as harassers or tormentors. They try to control by smooth talking, saying the right thing at the right time and lying. This type of bully gets his or her power through cunning, manipulation and deception. As different as these two types may seem, all bullies have characteristics in common, including:

- They are concerned with their own pleasure.
- They want power over others.
- They are willing to use and abuse other people to get what they want.
- They feel pain inside, perhaps because of their own shortcomings.

- They find it difficult to see things from someone else's perspective.

Bullies like to be in control of situations and enjoy inflicting pain on others. They are not committed to their school work or teachers and often show a lack of respect toward their families and adults at school. Usually bigger and stronger than other children their own age, bullies believe that their anger and violent behavior is justified. They see threats where none exist out of paranoia, or fear of facing reality.

The bully may lash out at people because he or she is angry about something. Maybe someone in his life is bullying him. He could be hurting from abuse received in the past, or maybe he grew up observing those around him using violence as a means of settling differences. Sometimes jealousy is the culprit. He needs to feel better about himself in order to change, and to stop bullying.

Or, in a worst case scenario, he might actually be a sociopath, in which case he or she would need professional assistance (Noll and Carter, 2001).

Not all bullies are obnoxious, threatening or meanies. Some are much more insidious, sneaking into a child's life as a friend who eventually pushes and prods a child to dress a certain way, behave badly or engage in illegal activities. Some bullies are girls. Or family members. Or teachers. And when children are bullied they sometimes turn into bullies themselves.

Bullies tend to be insecure with poor or non-existent social skills and little empathy. They turn this insecurity outwards, finding satisfaction in their ability to attack and diminish the capable people around them.

A bully can be convincing, a practiced liar and when made to account, will make up anything spontaneously to fit their needs at that moment. They also can have a Jekyll and Hyde nature: vile, vicious, and vindictive in private; innocent and charming in front of witnesses to the point that no one can believe this individual has a vindictive nature. Only the current target of the bully's aggression sees both sides. While the Jekyll side is charming and convincing enough to deceive others, the Hyde side is frequently described as evil; Hyde is the real person, Jekyll is an act.

Bullies can excel at deception and should never be underestimated in their capability to deceive. They use excessive charm and are very convincing when peers, parents and administrators are present.

Bullies can be control freaks and have a compulsive need to control everyone and everything. They also display a compulsive need to criticize while simultaneously refusing to value, praise and acknowledge others, their achievements or their existence.

A bully often has an overwhelming, unhealthy and narcissistic attention-seeking need to portray themselves as a wonderful, kind, caring and compassionate person in contrast to their behavior and treatment of others. Bullies see nothing wrong with their behavior and choose to remain oblivious to the discrepancy between how they like to be seen and how they really are seen by others.

Bullies often are convinced of their superiority and have an overbearing belief in their qualities of leadership but cannot distinguish between leadership (maturity, decisiveness, co-operation, trust, integrity) and bullying (immaturity, aggression, manipulation, distrust, deceitfulness).

The bully appears to lack insight into his or her behavior and seems to be oblivious to the crassness and inappropriateness. However, it is more likely that he or she are doing but elects to switch off the moral and ethical considerations by which normal people are bound.

Myth: Bullies are popular children.

Fact: Bullies are sometimes surrounded by other children not through popularity but through fear. The bully is rarely able to sustain a friendship (which is based on trust, dependability, loyalty and mutual respect) but instead forms alliances which are part of his or her strategy for power and control. A hard look at the bully and his or her cohorts will reveal a gang or clique mentality in which true friendship is absent. Some children side with the bully because they gain sufficient bravado to act like bullies themselves—which they are too weak and inadequate to do without the bully—but most children side with the bully for fear of otherwise becoming a target. Those children who do not join the gang or clique are then targeted by the bullies who gain strength from numbers.

Bullies tend to be glib, shallow and superficial with plenty of fine words and lots of form, but no substance. Therefore, they have nothing to offer in a friendship or a relationship. In a relationship they are incapable of initiating or sustaining intimacy. They are quick to belittle, undermine, denigrate and discredit anyone who calls, attempts to call, or might call the bully to account.

Myth: Bullies have low self-esteem.

Fact: Most bullies have average or above average self-esteem. They suffer from aggressive temperaments, a lack of empathy and poor parenting.

Students who engage in bullying behaviors seem to have a need to feel powerful and in control. They appear to derive pleasure from inflicting injury and suffering on others, seem to have little empathy for their victims and often defend their actions by saying that their victims provoked them in some way.

According to Batsche and Knoff (1994).

> Students who regularly display bullying behaviors are generally defiant or oppositional toward adults, antisocial, and apt to break school rules. In contrast to prevailing myths, bullies appear to have little anxiety and to possess strong self-esteem. There is little evidence to support the contention that they victimize others because they feel bad about themselves.

Also according to Batsche and Knoff (1994),

> Students who are victims of bullies are typically anxious, insecure and cautious, and suffer from low self-esteem, rarely defending themselves or retaliating when confronted by students who bully them. They may lack social skills and friends, and they are often socially isolated. Victims tend to be close to their parents and may have parents who can be described as overprotective. The major defining characteristic of victims is that they tend to be physically weaker than their peers— other physical characteristics such as weight, dress, or wearing glasses do not appear to be significant factors that can be correlated with victimization.

Myth: There's no law against bullying so it must be okay.

Fact: Increasingly, parents are turning to the law to protect their children from bullying. The parents of two children in a Roman Catholic school in Las Vegas sued the parents of seven other students, claiming those students had bullied the two youngsters for more than a year. Both students were sixth grade students at the school, which was not named as a defendant.

In California, children who are bullied by classmates can get stay-away orders issued against the aggressors. Passed in 1998, the law provides for stay-away orders that allow police officers to arrest violators for making telephone contact, mailing letters, or coming within a specified distance of the victim. Democratic state senator Sheila Kuehl, who co-sponsored the bill, said the law closes "a very important and problematic loophole" by specifying that minors can be covered by court orders.

During Christine O Gregorie's tenure as president of the National Association of Attorneys General (NAAG) in 1999–2000, she visited many schools and the issue of bullying and school violence was evident in Washington's schools. She spoke with educators and students and learned that a major cause of school violence was bullying, teasing , harassing, and tormenting students by other students. The results of her listening conferences and those held by her colleagues around the country were published in April 2000 in an NAAG report, *Bruised Inside: What Our Children Say About Youth Violence, What Causes It, and What We Need to Do About It.* "Bruised inside" is a term used by a middle school girl who spoke of the lasting emotional pain of being bullied. Bullying is pervasive and action has to be taken to stop it, the report stated. Gregorie formed a volunteer task force to investigate bullying. The task force recommended legislation to help equip schools with the necessary tools to mitigate youth violence. The bill requires school districts to adopt policies that prohibit bullying behavior and establish procedures for reporting and investigating such behavior. The bill also requires districts to provide training for school staff and volunteers.

Michigan's State Board of Education mandated that public schools institute an anti-bullying program. The goal is to promote a positive school atmosphere that fosters learning, and to create a safe and fear-free school environment in the classroom, playground and at school sponsored activities.

The South Carolina School Board Insurance Trust is protected for lawsuits that may come about because of a violent situation under the general liability. Schools can also be protected if they do everything they can to minimize the possibilities of such incidents.

Courts have found schools culpable in civil cases when they failed to protect children, and have handed down decisions awarding monetary damages to students bullied at school. An example is a lawsuit filed in Washington State by the parents of Mark Iversen, a high school senior who was bullied and harassed each day beginning in junior high school. He was finally physically assaulted in a classroom. The suit contends the school did not take any action to prevent or stop the bullying despite complaints because Iversen was believed to be gay (Davila, 1997).

Many states see anti-bullying legislation as the next step in school

violence prevention, since many of the perpetrators in violent incidents have been students who were teased or threatened by others.

In the spring of 2001, the Colorado Legislature enacted a law which
required all public school districts to adopt a specific policy concerning bullying prevention and education. The premise is that everyone
shares the responsibility to see that bullying does not occur and school
employees are required to act promptly.

More and more states are beginning to require schools to adopt
anti-bullying policies. New Hampshire and West Virginia also recently
passed legislation that makes it mandatory for schools to have anti-bullying policies. Massachusetts has allocated one million dollars to bully-
proof its schools. New Hampshire recently instituted a law that allows
local school boards to create anti-bullying policies and provide disciplinary procedures for students who subject others to insults, taunts
or challenges, whether verbal or physical in nature.

Currently Michigan law provides that students in grades six or
above can be suspended by the local school board for up to 180 days—
almost the entire school year — if they commit a physical assault at
school.

In Nebraska a bill (LB1083) requires public schools to set up anti-
bullying programs and requires parents to lock up guns in secure con-
tainers away from any children under 16. More than one lobbyist
representing Nebraska school interests called the anti-bullying law an
unfounded mandate for schools. Also, it was noted that a spokesperson from the Lincoln Public Schools stated that there was not any room
in the curriculum to teach anti-bullying material. There was a lot of
debate about the gun issue because some parents do allow their children to handle guns at an early age.

The fight over the anti-bullying bill in Olympia, Washington, has
been a useful reminder of the debate over what is constitutionally protected speech and what isn't. School bullying isn't. The bill would
require every school district to ban bullying. Most of the bigger districts— Seattle, Tacoma, Bellevue, Edmonds and others— do so already.
Others have no ban on bullying as such, though all have rules against
the physical aspect of it — hitting, kicking and shoving. It's the non-
physical part that causes arguments. The bill would require schools to
ban behavior, including speech, that seriously alarms, annoys, harasses
or is detrimental to the student, and which serves no legitimate pur-

pose and would cause a reasonable person to suffer emotional distress. It bans behavior, including speech, that has the effect of creating an intimidating, hostile or offensive environment for the students.

On October 23, 2000, in Manchester County (England) Court, a former grammar school pupil was awarded £1500 for damages after a judge found that Sale Grammar School had breached its duty of care for failing to protect the pupil against 18 months of verbal abuse and bullying which culminated in sexual assault on a school trip (Case law and settlements for school bullying web site).

On September 20, 1999, in *Carnell v. North Yorshire County Council*, the defendants paid £6000 for a court settlement in an action involving pupil bullying at Harrogate Grammar School. This was England's first legal victory since it became mandatory the same month for schools to have bullying policies. This sent a very clear message to all school governors, and those of Harrogate Grammar School in particular, that they have a responsibility to know when complaints of bullying are made and how they should handle them (Case law and settlements for school bullying).

A North Carolina father who alleged that school officials were indifferent to repeated physical attacks on his son by classmates was heard in civil court. Elmer W. Stevenson alleged that his son, Alex, was subjected to numerous beatings by classmates in the fall of 1998 while he was in the sixth grade at Williamston Middle School in the 4,600 student Martin County, N.C., district. Both a federal court and the 40th Circuit court rejected Mr. Stevenson's civil rights lawsuit. The appeals court ruled that there was no special relationship between the school district and the boy that required the district to protect him from harm by classmates. The father's appeal to the Supreme Court was *Stevenson v. Martin County Board of Education* (No. 00-1821).

In November 1996, in *Sharp v. London Borough of Richmond-upon-Thames*, Sebastain Sharpe, 20, accepted an out of court settlement of £30,000 for four years of bullying while he was at Shene School, Richmond, London. Mr. Sharp said he was regularly insulted, kicked and punched by other kids, who also tied him up with string during a four year campaign that started when he was 11 years old. The London Borough of Richmond-upon-Thames said it wanted to contest the allegation but the Borough's insurance company wanted it settled as quickly as possible (Case law and settlements for school bullying).

Myth: Bullies are tough people.

Fact: Bullies often want people to look up to them, and they try to achieve this by acting tough. Their behavior is usually initiated to create a status for themselves. They are often unhappy in school, immature and unpopular, but other kids may associate with them out of fear rather than friendship. In some children, bullying is part of an overall pattern of antisocial behavior and rule breaking.

Bullies are weak, cowardly and inadequate people who as adults cannot interact in a mature professional manner and have to resort to psychological violence (and, with child bullies, physical violence) to get their way. Only weak people need to bully. They show an arrested level of emotional development. While language and intelligence may appear to be that of an adult, the bully displays the emotional age of a five year old. Bullies are control freaks and they have a compulsive need to control everyone and everything they say, do, believe, and think. They also have a compulsive need to criticize others while simultaneously refusing to value, praise and acknowledge others, their achievements or their existence. Consistently, a bully will undermine and destroy anyone they perceive to be an adversary, a potential threat, or who can see through the bully's mask. Thus they are quick to discredit and neutralize anyone who can talk knowledgeably about antisocial or sociopathic behaviors.

At least six out of ten bullies go on to become criminals. There's much evidence to suggest that children who bully at school and who get away with it go on to be bullies in the workplace; bullying at work costs industry and taxpayers billions of dollars each year.

Myth: Bullies are born bullies.

Fact: The majority of bullying is a learned behavior, and much of the learning occurs in the child's home when the child sees that bullying tactics work to get their way.

A lot of children, when asked about bullying, have said that it's fun — almost a form of entertainment where other people who are bystanders are like the audience. This behavior has benefits for the bully and one of the greatest things we need to do is to diminish those benefits.

There is no one particular thing that turns a child into a bully. However, studies show that the problem is generally triggered by something at home in the youngster's environment. This could include having parents who are overly punitive or verbally or physically abusive. A bully could have been victimized himself, perhaps by a sibling or another child. It becomes very easy for a child to turn around and do to someone else what's been done to him because he knows exactly how it feels.

Parents may also breed a bully be being overly permissive. By giving in when a child is obnoxious or demanding, they send the message that bullying pays off. Children actually feel more secure when they know parents will set limits.

Myth: Schools don't allow bullying.

Fact: Many members of the present generation of adults working in schools consider bullying to be a normal part of growing up, a rite of passage, a developmental stage, boys being boys— they simply don't see it as an issue. Also, their plates are more than full already. As a society, we expect and demand so much from our schools.

The most common way that schools deal with bullying is to ignore it. Many teachers don't see anything wrong with bullying. One Columbine student reported, "Teachers would see them push someone into a locker, and they'd ignore it" (Prendergast, 1999). A junior at Columbine said, "I can't believe the faculty couldn't figure it out. It was so obvious that something was wrong" (Dube, 1999). In another study, teachers were only able to identify ten percent of the students who reported being a victim of a bully (Paulk et al., 1999). A prevailing attitude among some teachers is that those who get bullied probably had it coming to them.

Very few schools have a clear policy on the issue of bullying for teachers to follow. Bullying hasn't been identified as a real problem — no problem, no policy. Some staff don't respond because it hasn't been defined as part of their job description.

There could be recourse against the school if something is not done about bullies. If the nature and severity of bullying has produced significant physical and emotional distress, and if negligence on the part of the school system has been involved, a parent could seek legal counsel to determine if a legitimate case exists.

As the Maine Project Against Bullying reported (see Chapter One), more than a third of victims who sought help said the problem got worse or nothing happened. Almost 6 percent of the children surveyed didn't tell anyone they had been bullied. This perceived lack of assistance at school for victimized students gives the implicit message that these behaviors are acceptable. This is unacceptable and may have devastating results on the victims' feelings of self-worth and subsequently a school's climate.

Many incidents of bullying continue unnoticed by teachers and parents and even by classmates. While only 15 percent of parents know their child is being bullied and tried to help their children, one half of the parents do not realize their child is being bullied.

Student surveys reveal that a low percentage of students seem to believe that adults will help victims of bullies. Students feel that adult intervention is infrequent and ineffective, and that telling adults will only bring more harassment from bullies. Students report that teachers seldom or never talk to their classes about bullying (Charach, Pepler and Ziegler, 1995). School personnel may view bullying as a harmless rite of passage that is best ignored unless verbal and psychological intimidation crosses the line into physical assault or theft.

School bullying is everyone's business. It is unrealistic to expect that it can be eliminated totally. We can't eradicate the conditions that turn some children into bullies and others into targets. But if everyone concerned — teachers, school authorities, police, parents and children — is truly committed to zero tolerance, then there is solid evidence that the amount and the severity of bullying can be reduced dramatically.

The school should be a safe and positive learning environment for all students. In order to achieve this goal, schools should strive to:

- Reduce, if not eliminate, bully-victim problems among students in and outside of the school setting;
- Prevent the development of new bully-victim problems; and
- Achieve better peer relations at school and create conditions that allow, in particular, victims and bullies to get along and function better in and outside the school setting.

Two general conditions must exist in order to prevent bullying: (1) adults should be aware of the extent of bully-victim problems in their own schools; and (2) these adults should involve themselves in changing the situation.

Schools and classrooms should establish and stick to rules to prevent bullying. Adults must clearly and consistently communicate that bullying is not acceptable behavior. The following rules should apply to all students:

- We will not bully other students.
- We will try to help students who are bullied.
- We will make it a point to include all students who are easily left out.
- When we know someone is being bullied, we will tell a teacher, parent or adult we trust. (Students should be assured that telling an adult is not tattling, but instead that they are showing compassion for victims of bullying behavior.)

It is important to note that these rules target all students, not just the bullies or victims. The introduction of these rules establish classroom norms or structures that can contribute to the prevention of bullying.

Students tend to feel less safe and are less satisfied with school life in schools where bully-victim problems occur. In schools where bully-victim problems are ignored, students may start to regard this behavior as acceptable. This may result in more bullying behavior as well as other, possibly more severe, problems.

When teachers and administrators fail to intervene, some victims ultimately take things into their own hands, often with grievous results. In its recent analysis of 37 school shooting incidents, the U.S. Secret Service learned that a majority of the shooters had suffered "bullying and harassment that was longstanding and severe" (U.S. Secret Service National Threat Assessment Center, 2000).

As increasing amounts of research emerge about bullying effects on children — some of which can be devastating — adults are turning their heads toward the problem. But, too often, when teachers hear about bullying, they expect youngsters to work it out on their own. Telling the child to work it out doesn't address how powerless he is. By the time the child who's the victim is distressed or courageous enough to tell a teacher, the child doing the bullying has immense power. The bullying has been going on for a long period of time. As adults, we need to think about how to deal with this.

A point worth remembering is most students are neither bully nor victim. They are, however, witnesses to the bullying that takes place around them. Children's exposure to violence and maltreatment (including verbal abuse) of others is significantly associated with increased depression, anxiety, anger, post-traumatic stress, alcohol use and low grades. Given the frequency of bullying, it is important to acknowledge the effects of bullying on bystanders and the potential effects on school climate.

Myth: Bullying only takes place in schools in the United States.

Fact: Bullying in schools is a worldwide problem that can have negative consequences for the general school climate and for the right of students to learn in a safe environment without fear. Bullying can also have negative lifelong consequences— both for students who bully and for their victims. Although much of the research has taken place in the Scandinavian countries, Great Britain, and Japan, the problems associated with bullying have been noted wherever formal schooling environments exist.

Bullying by fellow classmates may be the most universal problem the schools have in common. Schools throughout the world experience bullying. Regardless of types of schools or nationalities—bullying is universally present.

In Japan, 51,544 incidents in 13,693 public schools during the 1996-1997 school year in compulsory education were reported for bullying. These numbers by no means show how widespread the problem is in private schools and the seriousness of bullying in Japan. According to the survey conducted by the Ministry of Education in 1997, among 30,000 public elementary and junior high school students, 32.1 percent of the students have experienced some sort of bullying.

In Finland one in ten children report being bullied weekly at school. Boys are involved in bullying, both as victims and as bullies, more often than girls. Primary school children are more likely to be victims of bullying than adolescents, but the number of bullies tends to remain constant between primary school and secondary school.

Researchers in New South Wales, Australia, conducted a study of 3,928 schoolchildren in three classes (ages 12, 14 and 16) in 115 schools. The children reported that in the previous school term, 24 percent had bullied others, 13 percent were bullied, 22 percent were also victims of bullying and 42 percent were neither bullied nor bullied others. Not surprisingly, the problem was more common among boys than it was among girls. It was concluded that bullies tended to be unhappy with school, while students who were bullied tended to like school but feel alone. Students who were both bullies and victims had the greatest number of psychological and psychomatic symptoms (Child Health Alert, 1999).

Evidence exists of considerable problems with bullies and bullied children in secondary schools. In the largest survey in the United Kingdom to date, ten percent of pupils reported they had been bullied sometimes or more often, while four percent reported being bullied at least once a week. The most common kind of bullying is name calling, followed by being hit, threatened or having rumors spread about oneself. Bullying is thought to be more prevalent among boys (Salmon, October 3, 1998).

Myth: Bullying is usually short-term, it doesn't last very long.

Fact: The duration of bullying varies. Bullying mostly lasts a week or so. But in some cases it last for months. Among the older students, bullying can last longer, sometimes over a year.

Olweus (1993) found there was a stability of bully-victim problems over time. Bullies and victims tend to perpetuate these roles throughout their school years. Harassing student behavior does not spontaneously appear in middle school. It has its origins in preschool. The current research regarding antisocial behavior makes clear that early intervention in home, school and the community are the best hope we have of diverting children from these behaviors.

A study published in the April 25 issue of the *Journal of the American Medical Association* examined bullying among sixth through tenth graders and found that bullies were more likely to drink and smoke. Other research has suggested that bullies are more likely to grow to abuse their spouses and are more likely to engage in criminal behavior. Specific studies are increasingly showing that bullying can have lifelong consequences that are not normal. People who are bullied often become bullies. People who are bullied can become killers. People who are bullied may kill themselves. Bullying on the playgrounds in elementary school may have a lifetime effect because when these bullies grow up, they may become spouse and children abusers. Therefore, bullying is a public health problem that merits our immediate attention.

In the short-term:
- Painful and humiliating experiences can cause victims to be unhappy, distressed and confused.
- Victims lose self-esteem and become anxious and insecure.
- Physical injury or threats of physical injury may affect concentration and learning and result in refusal to attend school.

- Victims may feel stupid, ashamed and unattractive and may start to view themselves as failures.
- Victims may develop psychosomatic symptoms such as stomach aches or headaches.
- Constant devaluation of themselves may lead to depression and suicide.

In the long-term:

- Students (particularly boys) who bully are more likely to engage in antisocial or delinquent behavior (vandalism, shoplifting, truancy, and drug use) into adulthood.
- Bullies are four times as likely as non-bullies to be convicted of crimes by age 24.
- Physical bullying is a moderate risk factor for serious violence at ages 15–25.

Myth: The best way to deal with bullying is to tell the victim to stand up for himself or herself.

Fact: It's strange that people tell you to stand up for yourself but then don't tell you how. Even adults find it difficult to defend themselves against the onslaught of a bully. They are powerfully propelled by anger and resentment, perhaps because of the way they are treated at home, and they may believe they are entitled to what they can get by unleashing their aggression on others. They are motivated by jealousy and envy to put down and control other children, because of their own incompetence or inadequacy. This is a hard cycle to break and it makes it even harder to stand up to the bully. Normally, when confronted, or if you tell an adult, the bully is slick enough to lie their way out of the situation. They excel at deception and should never be underestimated in their capability to deceive. Also, bullies are usually skilled in being able to anticipate what people want to hear and then saying it plausibly. The best advice — tell an adult when bullying occurs.

Myth: Bullying toughens you, makes a man (woman) out of you.

Fact: Bullying is in the same league as harassment, discrimination, racism, violence, assault, stalking, physical abuse, sexual abuse, molestation and rape. It causes trauma and psychiatric injury and can, if untreated, cause a psychiatric injury of sufficient seriousness to harm a person for life, causing a poorer standard of health and preventing them reaching their potential. The symptoms of psychiatric injury caused by bullying is consistent with post-traumatic stress disorder.

Myth: Bullying or being bullied is part of growing up.

Fact: Harassment, discrimination, racism, violence, assault, stalking, physical abuse, sexual abuse, molestation, rape and murder are all part of life but they are unacceptable.

Some people think bullying is just a part of growing up and a way for young people to learn to stick up for themselves. But bullying can make young people feel lonely, unhappy and frightened. It makes them feel unsafe and can leave them thinking there must be something wrong with them. They lose confidence and may not want to go to school anymore. It may make them sick.

Myth: People who get bullied are wimps.

Fact: People who are targeted by bullies are sensitive, respectful, honest, creative, have high emotional intelligence, a strong sense of fair play and high integrity with a low propensity to violence. Bullies (who lack these qualities) see these as vulnerabilities to be exploited. Sometimes, behind the stereotype, it is a child with a higher than average level of emotional maturity and a capacity to communicate maturely with adults.

Victims of bullies are usually younger than the bully and physically weaker. They also lack the social skills to develop supportive friendships and may be overprotected by their parents.

Bullies tend to zone in on individuals who appear vulnerable for some reason. Victims are usually passive, anxious, sensitive and quiet, or stand out in some way. At the same time, youngsters who are provocative and annoying, who seek negative attention from peers, also tend to get picked on. Both passive and aggressive victims tend to have few friends, and therefore few allies to rally to their defense in a sticky situation.

Generally there are two types of victims: (1) the passive or submissive victim, and (2) the provocative victim. Passive or submissive victims signal to others through attitudes and behaviors that they are insecure individuals who will not retaliate if victimized. The provocative victim is a much smaller group of victims. They are characterized by having both anxious and aggressive patterns. Provocative victims are generally boys.

Passive-submissive victims may:
- Be physically weaker than their peers (particularly boys).
- Display body anxiety. There are afraid of being hurt, have poor

physical coordination, and are ineffective in physical play or sports.
- Have poor social skills and have difficulty making friends.
- Be cautious, sensitive, quiet, withdrawn and shy.
- Cry or become easily upset.
- Be anxious, insecure and have poor self-esteem.
- Have difficulty standing up or defending themselves in peer groups.
- Relate better to adults than to peers.

Provocative victims may:
- Exhibit some or all of the characteristics of passive or submissive victims.
- Be hot tempered and attempt to fight back when victimized — usually not very effectively.
- Be hyperactive, restless, have difficulty concentrating and create tension.
- Be clumsy, immature and exhibit irritating habits.
- Be also disliked by adults, including teachers.

Myth: Maybe the victim deserves to be bullied — he or she antagonized the bully.

Fact: Perish the thought. A child never deserves to be bullied and intimidated by another. Remember, bullying is the willful, conscious desire to hurt another and put him or her under duress. Thus, bullying is seen as a desire, to hurt another human being. A common thread in all of the school shootings of the past two years is that all of the shooters had been bullied by their peers. So bullying may lead to other violent issues. Victims can eventually take revenge on their tormentors as well as others. In all of these situations there was a history of verbal abuse and ostracism perpetrated by peers, with school being the primary site of the antagonism.

Myth: Violence on television makes children turn into bullies.

Fact: The average elementary age child spends 30 hours per week viewing television. By 16, the average child will have witnessed 200,000 acts of violence and by 18, approximately 40,000 sexually explicit scenes (Garrett, 2001).

Ninety-eight percent of American homes have at least one television set, which is watched each week for an average of 28 hours by children between the ages of two and eleven, and 23 hours by teenagers (Garrett, 2001).

There are opposing viewpoints on this issue. A lot of people watch violence on television but not that many are violent. Therefore, television is not a uniform cause of bullying, otherwise, everyone who watched violence on television would be a bully. However, repeatedly watching scenes of violence and bullying can desensitize people, especially young people in their formative years. Violence is about power, and violence on television serves as a lesson of power that puts people in their places. We live in a world which is erected by the stories we tell and by extension, it is erected by the stories we are told. This is changing; the stories we are told now are not told to us by parents, school, church or community, but by a relatively small group of global conglomerates with something to sell. This alters in a fundamental way the cultural environment into which our children are born, grow up and become socialized.

Defenders of television argue that children are subject to violence and bullying in other media — including fairy tales and other literary classics.

— *How Popular Is Bullying in the Media?* —

Bullying has become such a hot topic that talk shows are actually advertising for participants. Recently on a web site (), the following advertisements were posted:

"MSNBC Investigator needs to find a victim of bullying who is willing to let them tag along with him/her during the school day. If you'd like to help get the word out and educate people on what is REALLY going on everywhere, please contact me."

"The Amanda Lewis Show is looking for girl victims to do a good show to help both."

"Inside Edition needs actual bullying caught on video (school or non-school related). School name doesn't need to be used and the kids/teens faces can be blurred out. They're also interested in law suits (previous or pending) as a result of bullying."

"Montel Williams Show needs kids who are bullied/teased and don't know what to do, and the extremes some have gone to, to prevent themselves and others from being picked on. Good show set up as a forum (no fighting) to help them and everyone watching. Children appearing as guests will not be exploited. Also, contact me if you are the parent of a bully and would like to help your child resolve these issues."

"I'm also working with CBS News show 48 Hours and MTV (Arnold Shapiro Productions) on documentaries to help bullies and victims. Honest and revealing — ultimately inspiring kids to think past the current moment and realize their actions have consequences that not only [affect] themselves but also their communities, classmates, friends and most importantly, the people they love."

Recent tragedies involving violence in schools across the nation have stemmed from bullying and revenge. The consequences of bullying are far-reaching and cause problem behaviors, poor psycho-social functioning, avoidance of school attendance, severe emotional problems (including suicide), and physical problems. Some students who observe unchallenged bullying behavior are likely to copy this anti-social behavior.

Chapter Three, Effects of Bullying, will discuss the victim and lasting effects of bullying. Bullying is a serious problem that can dramatically affect the ability of students to progress academically and socially.

Three

Effects of Bullying

If you were picked on as a kid, odds are you have never forgotten it. Teasing and taunting have always been viewed as a normal part of growing up. But recent incidents of school violence have focused new attention on an old problem and now educators say they can no longer ignore it.

Tragic, high profile school shootings across the nation over the past several years illustrate that the youth violence epidemic has broadened in terms of age, geography and sex to include all populations. The recent shootings in Williamsport, Pennsylvania (involving teenaged females as both victim and assailant), and Santee, California (involving a teenaged male assailant wounding or killing a dozen teenagers), have again raised a number of issues concerning early identification of violence risk factors and possible missed prevention opportunities.

Importantly, these recent tragedies and many previous episodes of school violence have involved the same issues of bullying and revenge. These issues have not been as prominent a part of the last two decades of public health efforts to prevent violence as they should. Violence prevention, including bullying as a component, must be a priority for all who are concerned about the health of children. Greater attention, energy and funding are required to include anti-bullying interventions in our schools.

The National Education Association states that "bullying, like its older cousin sexual harassment, needs to be addressed as a matter of social justice; it is an affront to democracy and to our democratic institutions. Bullying deprives children of their rightful entitlement to go to school in a safe, just and caring environment; bullying interferes with children's learning concentration and the desire to go to school" (Crawley, December 17, 1999).

The primary lesson is the use of power and aggression; those with power can be aggressive and being aggressive may enhance status. Some other lessons bullies and their victims learn are as follows:

- Lack of intervention implies that bullying is acceptable and can be performed without fear of consequences. If there are punishments, the responsibility is diffused among peers.
- Bullies learn that power and aggression lead to dominance and status. Peers learn to align with the dominant individual for protection and status.
- Victims may learn helplessness, submissiveness and negative means of gaining attention from peers. Peers learn to blame the victim.

A major concern is that lessons transfer to more serious forms of violence that continue to combine power and aggression in adolescence and into adulthood.

Victims

Victims of school bullies remember the pain forever. As one recalled:

"When I was at primary school I got picked on non-stop for two years. No one talked to me. I hadn't done anything to get blamed for, and I still don't know the reason I got picked on. I wasn't any wealthier or poorer or a different race.

"I used to cry myself to sleep every night. I was miserable. My parents knew and they talked to the headmaster but he wasn't interested and said he couldn't do anything about it. My parents knew all the bullies' parents. One girl even lived in the same street and we had been friends since we were two. Like a sheep, she dumped me because no one else talked to me.

"This all happened in primary 6 and I have lost all my self-confidence and hate being on my own. I'd hate to think this was happening to anyone else. I have a fear that if one girl doesn't talk to me they will all start again and it will never stop. I don't want it to go on for the rest of my life" (girl, age 14).

According to an abcnews.com report, "How to Battle the School Bully" (2000),

For the child who's been targeted by a bully, their life is a living hell," said Glenn Stutzky, a school violence specialist at Michigan State University. "Bullying is probably the most frequently occurring form of violence in American schools today and it's really the engine that drives the majority of violence. It's a huge problem [How to Battle the School Bully, 2000].

For Rachel Fannon, 16, being abused by her classmates in Littleton, Colorado, for five and a half years took both a physical and emotional toll. 'They had actually a contest: They'd high five each other if they come up with the best name how to describe how ugly I was,' she said. 'They'd kick me in the back of the knees and give me small bruises or they tripped me.' Fannon, who has a heart condition, would suffer attacks of rapid heartbeats after being harassed. Her grades dropped. She became withdrawn and had no friends. After school she would lock herself in her room and cry. 'All day, every day, they kept harassing me,' she said. 'Everywhere I went, they were there.' Fannon said teachers told her to tough it out or to ignore it. She said she was too embarrassed to tell her parents, but she finally confided in her mother. Principals of her school said the complaints never reached them, but they admit that despite their anti-bullying policies, Fannon somehow fell through the cracks [How to Battle the School Bully, 2000].

Despite being 6 feet and 200 pounds, Chris Velasquez, now 14, said he was beaten so badly at his middle school that he was taken to the emergency room. 'They caught me in the stairway and jumped me and I couldn't see anything,' he recalled. 'I had one kid punching me a lot of times in the face, and one just repeatedly hitting me in the back.' Though the incident was reported to school authorities, Velasquez said the boys who beat him up were not even suspended. His family is now suing the school district [How to Battle the School Bully, 2000].

James Bricker, a 77 year old Leesville resident, recalls how one football player made a practice of bullying him in 1942. Years later the bully died after a fall from a water tower, but Bricker suspects "that he was pushed off by some little man that he picked on" (Gregory, 2001). Bricker says the memories are fresh, although the bullying happened almost 60 years ago. Whether decades ago or just last year, bullying is painful for the victims and parents who try to shield their children from it.

Watching her child tortured by bullies was agonizing for one Rapides Parish parent. She advised her preteen daughter to ignore the bullies, a group of girls, who teased her because she wasn't sexually active. Trying to win over the bullies with friendship didn't work either; her daughter's possessions were stolen. In frustration, the parent finally told her daughter to fight back. It's a decision she regrets now, though her daughter never became involved in physical violence. But bullying can lead to physical violence, sometimes with deadly consequences (Gregory, 2001).

Pam Blackmon says her son was bullied for several years in school because of his race. Her son, who is white, attended a majority black elementary school in Alexandria. Like the bullied girl's mother, Blackmon told her son to fight back after her pleas for help were ignored. Blackmon said her son was verbally and physically bullied by a group of boys beginning in the second grade. She said her son was beaten up in second grade and was choked to near unconsciousness when he was in the third grade. The child started to hate school. The bullying made her son prejudiced. Mrs. Blackmon says she talks to her son to help him through his emotions, but she worries. She spoke with her son's teachers and they agreed that her son was being bullied. She said school officials did not help or stop the bullying. The only person that helped look out for her son was the janitor. Blackmon said her son has become more physically aggressive and more likely to defend himself (Gregory, 2001).

In victims, bullying is associated with physical harm, low self-esteem, anxiety, depressed mood, tiredness, illness, and lack of concentration. Other side effects might include reduced academic performance, loneliness, unhappiness at school, disruptive behavior, truancy and an inability to form relationships. Virtually every person who has been to school has either seen or experienced some bullying. We are each affected by it.

Children who are bullied will have short-term and long-tern negative responses. If the child is hurt and shamed over and over and can't work out those feelings out, it may lead to violence.

"How to Battle the School Bully" (2000) also says To deal with being bullied, some children seek revenge. Velasquez can understand. "I do think about going into school and doing something," he said. "But then I think what will that make me look like? A criminal" (How to Battle the School Bully, 2000).

Other children turn their anger inward. Each year, one out of 13 kids under the age of 19 attempts suicide, a rate that has tripled over the last 20 years. Last year, more than 2,000 of them succeeded — a staggering number in which bullying can be blamed as a factor. Glenn Stutzky said, "We're not even realizing the fact that suicide is bully's quiet little secret. It's picking off our children one at a time" (How to Battle the School Bully, 2000).

Eleven year old Eric Smith killed a schoolmate in Texas after enduring years of systematic and constant abuse through bullying and harassment at school. The kind of less than extreme physical and emotional abuse that Eric experienced is debilitating and can lead to frustration and more violence. Bullying, as a specific form of violence, has been defined as repeated oppression, psychological or physical, of a less powerful person by a more powerful person or group of persons.

Another example from "How to Battle the School Bully" (2000) is also illustrative:

> Twelve year old Tempest Smith was one of them from the time she was in the second grade, said her mother Danessa Smith. Tempest was the brunt of cruel jokes and constant humiliation. One time, recalls Smith, a group of kids pretending to be Tempest's friends came over to her house, only to ransack her room. Tempest would also be pushed in the lunch line, and her classmates would purposely knock things off her desk. Smith said the school wouldn't do anything about it and would not acknowledge the problem. By the time Tempest reached seventh grade, Smith was so fed up that she planned to home-school her daughter. But she never got that chance. On February 20, Tempest took her life. Smith is now suing the school district, which has denied any wrongdoing [How to Battle the School Bully, 2000].

In March 2000, an honor roll student named Hamed Nastoh jumped off the Pattullo Bridge in New Westminister, B.C. Hamed, 14, left a seven page letter that said he was killing himself because his classmates tormented him with names like gay or faggot. He had never told his mother he was being bullied.

A few months later, on November 10, 2000, another 14 year old, Dawn Marie Wesley of Mission, B.C., hanged herself with a dog leash in her bedroom. She too left a note for her family. The note said things had gotten worse and the girls were always looking for a new person to beat up. She was afraid to tell anyone because of retaliation.

Lienert (2001) offers this example:

> Tricia Couture, a senior at Eastern Michigan University, was an eight year old third grader when the bullying began. She was a shy, bookish child who wore her sister's hand-me-down clothing instead of the more trendy clothes. "If you didn't have the right clothes, it automatically excluded you," Couture, now 22, says. "I read at recess instead of playing. No one would talk to me anyway. In fourth grade, I started having acne, so the kids called me 'pizza face.' The name calling went on through high school.... My parents told me to ignore them. That doesn't work. But I don't know what else they could have done."

The National School Safety Center in Westlake Village, California, reports that bullying is the most enduring and underrated problem in American schools. But in the years since the massacre at Columbine High School in Littleton, Colorado, bullying has had increasingly fatal consequences.

Charles Andrew Williams (2001), the fifteen year old who opened fire from a bathroom at Santana High in Santee, California, on March 5, killing two and wounding 13, was bullied. So was Elizabeth Catherine Bush (2001), 14, who took her father's revolver to Bishop Neumann, a small Roman Catholic Church school in Williamsport, Pennsylvania, on March 7 and shot another girl in the shoulder. In three-quarters of recent shootings, the assailants say they were taunted or picked on by classmates, according to the United States Secret Service.

The Michigan Education Association, the state's largest teachers' union, defines bullying as physical intimidation, verbal behavior that includes teasing, name-calling and rumors or emotional intimidation, such as excluding a child form a group activity. They also cite bullying as contributing to school violence.

Teasing and bullying are part of daily life for students in kindergarten through third grade, according to a recent study by Educational Equity Concepts and the Wellesley College Center for Research on Women. The study noted teachers and other adults ignore 71 percent of the observed incidents of bullying, thus giving approval to aggressive behavior.

Most Canadians remember the tragic 1997 murder of Reena Virk, a high school student whose battered body was recovered from the Gorge Waterway, near Victoria, British Columbia. Her head and internal organs had been severely damaged by a beating that rendered her senseless before she was deliberately drowned. One girl and a boy were convicted of second degree murder, and six girls were found guilty of aggravated assault. Her death is an example of bullying taken to its ultimate expression. But even in its mildest everyday forms, bullying is about one thing: the strong taking unfair advantage of the weak.

Patrick Smith (not real name) is a happy-go-lucky seven year old in second grade at a small elementary school near Halifax. His parents say Patrick loves everybody and talks to everyone. But shortly after the school year started Patrick starting crying at night and did not want to go to school anymore. With a lot of coaxing, Patrick told his parents the problem — an older second grade boy was spitting on him every morning as he got on the bus. Patrick's parents spoke to the bus driver but didn't get any help. The spitting on Patrick continued so his parents talked to the bus driver for a second time. The bus driver moved Patrick to the front of the bus—away from the second grader. The spitting continued and Patrick continued crying and not wanting to go to school. Patrick's parents tried to talk to the bully's parents. The boy's father met them on the doorstep. He listened then told them Patrick must have done something to deserve it. He then became belligerent. Patrick's parents walked away thinking they knew how the child became a bully. In desperation, they told Patrick to spit back if he was spit on. The next morning Patrick was spit on and he did spit back. The incident was solved and the spitting was stopped. This is a very unusual case with positive results. Sometimes striking back or retaliating does not help, but it makes the situation worse.

The next example comes from the School Violence: Bullying website:

> I was shocked to learn that the Santee shooting of March 5 seems to have had its roots in bullying. The 15 year old who allegedly killed two students and wounded 13 others feared for his life and was determined to do something about it. I personally remember being terrified of bullies when I was 10 to 12 years old. But using a gun or even resorting to physical or verbal violence with the situation simply did not occur to me. It still wouldn't. It got me thinking about how I react to situations where I feel threatened. My bully turned out to be somewhat infamous. Mr. Bully lived across the street from me. He taunted me and teased me. I was very sensitive, rather puny kid who spent all of my time playing the piano and reading. I did not like sports and was very shy with people I didn't know. Mr. Bully knew I was vulnerable and took great delight in threatening me. I don't recall his actually hitting me, but I was very uncomfortable when I saw him outside his house, as I knew that I'd be subjected to some kind of verbal abuse. The fact that I remember this experience to this day proves how humiliating and demeaning bullying can be [School Violence: Bullying web site]. Robert Kennedy.

The effects of school bullying can be devastating. Students who are bullied suffer from low self-esteem, often have poor concentration and may refuse to continue in school. Bullied students tend to feel stupid, ashamed, unattractive and gradually begin to view themselves as failures. Many victims develop psychosomatic symptoms such as headaches and stomach pains. These feelings can become overwhelming and children can begin to see suicide as the only possible solution.

Other students who have been bullied see a gun and random shooting as the only way to balance the asymmetrical power relationship.

Jim Unnever, a sociology professor at Radford University in Virginia, conducted a study in the Roanoke City Schools. He concludes that bullying is part of a more general antisocial and rule-breaking behavior pattern. Students, especially boys, who bully are more likely to engage in other antisocial and delinquent behaviors such a vandalism, shoplifting, truancy and drug use. This antisocial behavior continues to adulthood. In fact, 60 percent of boys who were characterized as bullies in grades six through nine are convicted of at least one crime by the age of 24. He further elaborates that schools need early intervention programs. We know children are bullied in our schools, their self-esteem is damaged in the process and some type of violence is likely to result. He suggests that we err on the side of caution and not wait for the shock we know is coming (Shareef, 2002) .

Who Becomes a Victim?

Children who become repeated victims of aggression tend to be quiet and shy in temperament. They tend not to retaliate or make any assertive responses to the initial aggression, which is then repeated by the bully. Children who become victims typically lack friends and social support at school, and they are often not confident in their physical abilities and strength.

Some children actually seem to provoke their own victimization. These children will tease bullies, make themselves a target by egging the person on, not knowing when to stop and then not being able to effectively defend themselves when the balance of power shifts to the bully.

While most victims do not do anything to provoke the victimization, there is a subgroup of victims who tend to show irritating and inappropriate social behavior. These children tend to be impulsive and have poor social skills. These provocative victims may also try to bully other children, so they are both bully and victim (Olweus, 1993).

Every morning there are students who dread the approaching school bus and the school day beginning. These are the children positioned on the bottom of the rung of the social ladder, the victims of the bullies. Long term effects on a child bombarded with insults and taunts can include diminishing self-esteem, declining grades, dropping out of school, and depression. Victims of prolonged bullying will eventually become either withdrawn or aggressive; in extreme cases suicidal or violently retaliatory.

A child suffering from constant harassment might think his actions caused the bully to single him out. He can blame himself for the bully's behavior. Often a child at the mercy of the playground bully will fail to report the abuse, fearing retaliation.

Few adults would tolerate bullying by their peers. After all, adults would expect support from several sources, including the law or an employees' union. Most adults also would have the psychological stamina to face up to unreasonable, overly aggressive behavior.

Children, on the other hand, have no such recourse. As a result, they suffer in more ways than the obvious scrapes and bruises might suggest. A child who is prey for the school bully may be stigmatized by other children as well, further eroding an already battered confidence. As a result, he may assume an attitude of self-reproach.

Bullying is frequently mentioned as a possible contributor to school violence. A report by the U.S. Secret Service notes that in more than two thirds of school shootings, the attackers experienced some form of bullying prior to the incident, and several attackers had experienced bullying at school over a long period of time. Not surprisingly, a CNN Gallup poll taken after the shootings at Columbine High School reported that most high school students blame each other for the bullying, teasing and harassment that pushes the Eric Harrises and Dylan Klebolds of the world over the edge (Lindsey, 2001) and though certainly not every child who is bullied will engage in serious violent acts, bullying is one of the most common forms of victimization at school.

It is important to emphasize that bullying is not a factor in every case of school violence.

Victims tend to fall into two categories: those who are provocative, and those who are passive. The passive victims are anxious, insecure, cry easily when attacked, and avoid confrontation. They may be smaller and weaker than their counterparts, and always have trouble standing up to the bully.

The provocative victims account for a small number of bullied children. These students may have a learning disability, and lack social skills that would allow them to interpret body language and facial expressions. Behaviors of these children send messages that create uneasiness. Because of this cognitive deficit, provocative victims will tease and annoy their classmates until someone lashes out at them. Unfortunately, teachers can mistake this skill deficit solely for repeated misbehavior, and often dislike these children. Social skills training can be extremely beneficial for this type of student.

What Does Bullying do to a Child's Health?

Bullying causes injury to health and can make one ill. Listed are some symptoms which may occur:
- Constant high levels of stress and anxiety;
- Frequent illnesses such as viral infections, especially flu and glandular fever, colds, cough, or chest, ear, nose and throat infections;
- Aches and pains in the joints and muscles with no obvious cause; also back pain with no obvious cause and which won't go away or respond to treatment;
- Headaches and migraines;
- Tiredness, exhaustion, constant fatigue;
- Sleeplessness, nightmares, waking early, waking up more tired than when you went to bed;
- Flashbacks and replays, obsessiveness, can't get the bullying out of your mind;
- Irritable bowel syndrome;
- Skin problems such as eczema, psoriasis, athlete's foot, ulcers, shingles;
- Poor concentration;
- Bad or intermittently functioning memory, forgetfulness, especially with trivial day-to-day things;
- Sweating, trembling, shaking, palpitations, panic attacks;
- Bursting into tears regularly and over trivial things;
- Uncharacteristic irritability and angry outbursts;
- Being constantly on edge;
- Hypersensitivity, fragility, isolation; and
- Shattered self-confidence.

The primary prevention of bulling or being bullied involves eliminating factors that promote such behaviors (risk reduction) and teaching children the skills for more prosocial interpersonal interaction (resiliency development). Understanding how to respond to bullying in an effective manner provides the opportunity to learn more about how to address the consequences of experiences with violence.

Psychological Effects on the Victim

As one middle school student expressed it, "There is another kind of violence, and there is violence by talking. It can leave you hurting more than a cut with a knife. It can leave you bruised inside (U.S. Secret Service National Assessment Center, 2000).

The psychological scars left by bullying often endure for years. Evidence indicates that the feelings of isolation and the loss of self-esteem that victims experience seem to last into adulthood (Clarke and Kiselica, 1997). Studies have found a higher level of depression and lower self-esteem among formerly bullied individuals at age twenty-three, even though as adults these individuals were no more harassed or socially isolated than a control group (Nansel, 2001).

When students are allowed to abuse power and bully others, a climate develops similar to one in an abusive home. Continual emotional stress can create deficits in a child's intellectual abilities, crippling the capacity to learn. A child always under stress will be robbed of his or her potential. How can students immerse themselves in projects if they always have to watch their backs? Bullying is likely to interfere not only with children's academic development, but also with their social and personal development. Victims of bullies often become socially isolated.

Children who are not bullied tend to have better social skills and conflict management skills. They are more willing to assert themselves about differences without being aggressive or confronting. They suggest compromises and alternative solutions. They tend to be more aware of people's feelings and are children who can be most helpful in resolving disputes and assisting other children to get help.

Psychological effects on the victim might include:
- Fear of going to the bathroom or other less supervised areas at school.
- Fear of the bus ride to and from school.
- Declining grades because attention is drawn away from learning.

- Fear that leads to absenteeism, truancy or dropping out of school.
- Losing or failing to develop self-esteem, experiencing feelings of isolation or becoming withdrawn and depressed.
- Hesitation in taking social, intellectual, emotional or vocational risks, as students and late as adults.
- If the problem persists, victims occasionally feel compelled to take drastic measures, such as vengeance in the form of fighting back, weapon carrying or even suicide.

Consequences of Being a Victim

Experiences of being bullied appear to have long-term effects on children, including lowered self-esteem, increased absenteeism, depression and suicide. Research on abuse within families consistently demonstrates that the abused are likely to become abusers when they have families of their own, leading to the suggestion that children who are bullied are more likely to become bullies themselves. Garbarino (1999) has suggested that boys bully to compensate for their experiences of victimization at home. A study of eight to twelve year old Finnish children indicated that those who were victims of bullying were often found to be involved in bullying four years later (Kumpalainen, Rasanen and Henttonen, 1999).

Adults, like children, resent being bullied, except that adult victims have more options for recourse available to them than do child victims. Children cannot escape the schoolyard, the hallway, or the bathroom. Sometimes, victims do not survive the torture and humiliation of bullying. In most situations, victims do survive, but carry their emotional scars for a lifetime.

By senior high school, regular bullying incidents are often a thing of the past, but all victims know who the bullies are, and avoid them. By age 16 or 17, bullies and victims are usually moving in different directions in terms of curricular interests in school, therefore their paths rarely cross. Social circles are clearly defined by this time in a student's life and invisible boundaries have been drawn.

When a child has been repeatedly victimized, certain behaviors and attitudes tend to emerge which are inconsistent with his or her typical behaviors. Often children are too embarrassed and humiliated to report victimization.

A School for Bullying Victims

A school which consists of 10 students has been set up for the victims of bullying. The Red Balloon Learning Centre in Cambridge, England, is seeking to provide a safe and reassuring environment for students who have been regularly bullied in their own schools. As well as academic lessons, students are given counseling and support designed to restore their confidence. Students are encouraged to talk about their experiences, which have often involved prolonged periods of physical and verbal assaults.

The school's youngest student, eleven year old Juliet Chippendale, recalled the sense of isolation when there was "no one to talk to" about the teasing that took place at her old school.

Westhead (2000) reports on the success of one boy's experience:

> Peter Parnwell, a fifteen year old, attempted suicide after two years of regular attacks, during which he suffered black eyes and broken bones. "I know what other children are going through, because I've been there myself. There is a way out, but you have to have somewhere like this to come to."

The school's founder, Carrie Herbert, says that she set up the school because she discovered there was no place for students who were too scared to attend their own school. "Students come here damaged. We take that damaged child and we nurture them as if they were in an intensive care incubator in a hospital. We listen to them, we believe them, we trust them," said Ms. Herbert (Westhead, 2000).

Bullies

"I have never actually set out to bully someone myself. It usually comes about when someone is being annoyed and provides an amusing reaction that I begin to join in. At the time you do not see it as bullying, although you may have doubts later. I do not think there is anyone at school who has not bullied someone in one way or another" (boy, 16, Supporting Schools Against Bullying: The Second SCRE Anti-Bullying Pack, 1993).

While active and assertive play is a normal sign of childhood, especially in boys, bullies are distinct in their quickness to begin a fight.

Belligerence, use of force and intimidation are the means bullies use to get their way. They are overly aggressive, destructive and enjoy dominating other children. According to the book *Social Development in Young Children* (Roedell et al. 1977), children learn to perform aggressive behaviors such as kicking, hitting and biting, and they learn to identify situations where these behaviors will have rewarding results.

Bullies see the world with a paranoid's eye. They see threats where there are none and they take these imagined threats as provocations to strike back. By the age of seven or eight, bullies are in the habit of misinterpreting an innocent brush or bump as a blatant attack. As a result, they feel justified in retaliating for what actually is an imaginary harm.

Bullies don't realize how aggressive they are. Bullies habitually perceive other children as being more aggressive than themselves. Bullies see their anger as justified and they see other children as having started the trouble.

If bullying behaviors are allowed to continue, they can escalate into even more serious behavior, such as sexual harassment or criminal activity in higher grades and adulthood. Furthermore, bullies are at an even greater risk of suicide than their victims, and often grow up to perpetuate family violence.

Who Are the Bullies?

Bullies are very often children who have been bullied or abused themselves. Sometimes they are children experiencing life situations that they cannot cope with, that leave them feeling helpless and out of control. They may be children with poor social skills, who do not fit in, or who can't meet the expectations of their family or school. They bully to feel competent, successful, to control someone else, to get some relief from their own feelings of powerlessness.

The best documented individual child factor in bullying is temperament. Temperament refers to basic tendencies by children to develop certain personality styles and interpersonal behaviors. Children who are active and impulsive in temperament may be more inclined to develop into bullies. With boys, physical strength compared to peers also seems to be a characteristic which is associated with bullying, although of course there are many strong, physically adept boys who never bully.

The typical bully is embittered by an abusive upbringing, seething with resentment, and irritated by others' failure to fulfill his or her superior sense of entitlement. They are fueled by anger resulting from rejection. The bully displays an obsessive, compulsive and self-gratifying urge to displace their uncontrolled aggression onto others while exhibiting an apparent lack of insight into their behavior and its effect on people around them. Jealousy and envy motivate the bully to identify a competent individual who is then controlled and subjugated through projection of the bully's own inadequacy or incompetence. When the victim asserts their right not to be bullied, a paranoid fear of exposure compels the bully to perceive that person as a threat and neutralize and dispose of them as quickly as possible. When the bully tires of one victim, he chooses another target, there's an interval of between two days and two weeks before the bully chooses another target and the cycle continues.

A bully as young as eight years old who is not taught how to behave and cope with frustration is very likely headed for a lifetime of failure, exacting a great toll from society. A disproportionately high number of these children underachieve in school or drop out, perform below potential throughout their careers, land in prison for committing adult crimes, and become abusive spouses and parents. Worst of all, they frequently raise a new generation of bullies, perpetuating the cycle of violence.

The bully is able to exert a hold over people for a variety of reasons. Victims are disempowered such that they become dependent on the bully to allow them to get through each day without their life being a living hell. The bully is often able to convince a colleague to supporting him or her; this person then becomes the bully's spokesperson and advocate. People are easily and repeatedly taken in by the bully's glib charm, Jekyll and Hyde nature, and constant lying.

Bullying is a conscious, willful and deliberate hostile act intended to harm, induce fear through the threat of further aggression, and create terror. Whether it is premeditated or seems to come out of the blue, is obvious or subtle, in your face or behind your back, easy to identify or cloaked in the garb of apparent friendship, done by one kid or a group of kids, bullying will always include these elements:
- Imbalance of power;
- Threat of further aggression; and
- Intent to harm.

When bullying escalates unabated, a fourth element is added:
• Terror.

Once terror is created, the bully can continue without fear of recrimination or retaliation. The bullied child is unlikely to fight back or tell anyone about the bullying. The bully counts on bystanders to participate in or support the bullying, or at least do nothing to stop it. The cycle of violence begins.

Bullying is systematic violence used to intimidate and maintain dominance. Terror struck in the heart of the child targeted isn't only a means to an end, it is an end in itself (Coloroso, 2002).

Consequences of Being a Bully

Adults who admit to having bullied others at school frequently experience a greater degree of depression than is found among adults who did not bully. Also, children who have been identified as school bullies have a much higher chance of later committing delinquent acts. As previously mentioned, Olweus (1993) reported in one study that 60 percent of students identified as bullies in grades six through nine had a criminal conviction by age 24. In this study, as many as 40 percent of former bullies had at least three convictions by age 24, whereas only 10 percent of boys who were neither bullies nor victims had convictions. Coincidentally, Garbarino (1999) reported that there are accounts of Mitchell Johnson (Jonesboro, Arkansas), Andrew Wurst (Edinboro, Pennsylvania) and Kip Kinkel (Springfield, Oregon) bullying other youngsters prior to bringing a gun to school and killing classmates.

The effects of bullying last a lifetime. It causes misery for the bully's victims, and leaves a lasting impression on all those who witness repeated bullying incidents. The lifelong outlook for bullies is not good. If bullies don't learn how to change their behavior, the pattern of bullying behavior often becomes a habit as the bully gets older.

Bullies have average social popularity up to approximately age 14 or 15. In fact, some children even look up to bullies in some ways because they are powerful and do what they want to, or have to, to get their way with their peers. However, by late adolescence, the bully's popularity begins to wane. By senior high school, if a bully is still attending school, his or her peer group includes other bullies, or more seriously, he or she has developed or is developing gang alliances. By late high school, schoolyard bullying is a rare occurrence, but what takes place is more serious.

A study by psychologist E. Eron at the University of Michigan spanning 35 years found that children who were named by their schoolmates, at age eight, as the bullies of the school were often bullies throughout their lives. In this longitudinal study, many of these children, as adults, required more support from government agencies. For example, these children later had more court convictions, more alcoholism, more antisocial personality disorders and used more of the mental health services than the other children.

Unless new behaviors are learned and adopted, bullies continue to bully throughout their lifetime. They bully their mates, their children and possibly people in the workplace. Bullying gets them what they want, and some bullies learn to refine the art of bullying in their professional lives and use it in situations where there is a power imbalance, which creates less than harmonious relations in the workplace.

What Are the Long Term Consequences for Victims and Bullies?

Victims of bullying typically are very unhappy children who suffer from fear, anxiety and low self-esteem as a result of the bullying. They may try to avoid school, and to avoid social interaction, in an effort to escape the bullying. Some victims of bullying are so distressed that they commit, or attempt to commit suicide. Several instances of suicide by boys who had been severely bullied occurred in Norway in the early 1980s. Children who are routinely bullied spend their childhood plagued by anxiety, insecurity and low self-esteem. Chronic victims of bullying need professional help as much as the bullies do.

Even when bullying does not drive victims to the extremes of suicide, victims experience significant psychological harm which interferes with their social, academic and emotional development. The sooner the bullying is stopped, the better the long term outcome for victims. If bullying patterns are allowed to continue unchecked, there are long term consequences for the victim. A follow-up study by Olweus (1993) found that by the time former male victims of bullying were in their early twenties, they had generally made a positive social adjustment, as they had more freedom to choose their social and work milieu. However, they were more likely to be depressed, and had lower self-esteem than a comparison group who had not been bullied.

Though being a bully has its power in elementary school, if that behavior continues, it is detrimental to the person as an adult. They may become outcasts as adults and may not be treated well for the rest of their adult lives. There are consequences for children who engage in bullying behavior and are encouraged in this by their parents. Working with parents of bullies can be a big challenge. Bullies tend to model behavior learned at home. Parents of victims should seek out parents of bullies that this behavior is unacceptable in school and there are consequences for it. The school environment has to be safe for everybody.

The serious long-term consequences for bullies are also important to recognize. Bullies tend to become aggressive adults who stand a much higher chance of obtaining multiple criminal convictions. These findings by Olweus and his group fit well with other studies which have found exactly the same outcome for adults, especially males, who are aggressive as children. Bullies are angry kids who usually are bullied at home by parents, step-parents, or older, bigger siblings. Bullies generally come from families where parents use physical means of discipline. They may be kids reacting poorly to divorce, death or other family crisis. However, bullying is not normal behavior and should not be dismissed as such.

Bystanders and Peers

Another important but often overlooked group of children who are affected by bullying are those children who are neither victims nor perpetrators, but who see bullying happening to their peers. There are also children who will not take the initiative themselves to bully, but will follow a bully's lead in helping harass or victimize a particular child in their class or school. All children, including bystanders, are negatively affected when bullying occurs. The bullying may cause anxiety or fear in bystanders. The learning environment is poisoned by bullying, particularly where there are no effective interventions. Children who observe violent behavior and see that it has no negative consequences for the bully will be more likely to use aggression in the future. Some experts suggest that changing attitudes and involvement of kids who witness but are not victims of bullying may have the greatest impact on bullies (Pitzer, 1992). Since bullies love an audience, a bystander's encouragement or toleration of the bully will make the bully stronger. Training through role-playing can help children recognize a potentially harmful situation and assertively do something positive. By simply saying it's not fun, a bystander can stop a bully's activities. Children need to know that taking a stand for what is right can be very effective.

Peers play a central role in the problem of bullying. Peers can be a positive influence in stopping bullying. Their role in addressing the problems in schools is critical, as they are always present and occasionally intervene, whereas adults seldom witness and intervene in bullying.

Research has shown:

- 11 percent of children reported they almost always tried to stop bullying; peers intervened in 11 percent of playground episodes.
- When peers intervene, they are successful in stopping bullying about half of the time. Without guidance, however, they are just as likely to intervene aggressively as prosocially. A focus intervention, therefore, is to teach the children appropriate ways to handle the situation.
- 80 percent to 90 percent of peers report it is unpleasant to watch bullying.
- Peers are present in 85 percent of the bullying episodes on the playground and in the classroom.
- One third of the children report they could join in bullying someone they didn't like.
- Peers assume many roles in bullying: co-bullies, supporters, audience and those who intervene.

Peer contributions to bullying and victimization may include the following:

- Peers are drawn into bullying interactions by arousal and excitement of aggression. Peers are the audience for the theatre of bullying.
- Positive attention, alignment, imitation, and lack of opposition reinforce the bully's dominance.

- Lack of empathy and intervention, negative attention, and attributions of blame substantiate the victim's role.
- Peers who align with the bully may become desensitized and aggressive. They may experience protection and increased social status. Group cohesion develops through a coordinated attack.
- There is a risk for peers who align with the victim. They could be the next victim.

Bystanders and peers of victims can be distracted from learning as well. They may:
- Be afraid to associate with the victim for fear of lowering their own status, inviting retribution from the bully, or becoming victims themselves;
- Fear reporting bullying incidents because they do not want to be called a snitch;
- Experience feelings of guilt or helplessness for not standing up to the bully on behalf of their classmate;
- Be drawn into bullying behavior by peer pressure;
- Feel unsafe and unable to take action, or fear a loss of control;
- Feel anger and helplessness for not knowing what to do;
- Have nightmares about being the next victim; or
- Fear certain areas in the school.

——— *A Public Health Concern* ———

Bullying is widespread in our schools, creating a public health problem that impacts both victims and perpetrators later in life.

"Being bullied is not just an unpleasant rite of passage through childhood," said Duane Alexander, director of the National Institute of Child Health and Human Development, which conducted research on 16,686 students in public and private schools from grades six through ten.

"It's a public health problem that merits attention," he said. "People who bullied as children are more likely to suffer from depression and low self-esteem, well into adulthood, and the bullies themselves are more likely to engage in criminal behavior later in life." The study, published in the *Journal of the American Medical Association* (November 7, 2001), comes at a time when deadly school shootings in the United

States have focused renewed attention on the roots and causes of violence. (Study: Bullying Common in Schools).

The school staff is generally unaware of the extent of bullying and victimization problems. Pepler (2000) reports that 42 percent of bullies and 46 percent of victims report they have talked to teachers about bullying problems. However, 71 percent of teachers and 25 percent of students say teachers almost always intervene. Lower teacher intervention may occur because the majority of episodes are verbal, episodes are brief, or bullying occurs when monitoring is low.

— *Acknowledging Bullying as a Crime?* —

Although bullying is not labeled a crime as such, bullying is a crime because it injures, maims, destroys and kills as effectively as a gun. Until a proactive approach is taken with bullying, a reactive approach to the crime of school shootings is futile.

Bullying is a crime in which the perpetrators are rarely punished and the victims rarely receive justice. This crime is usually repetitive — a victim is injured and traumatized over and over. Yet, bullying is rarely acknowledged as a crime. Usually the victims are blamed because they must have been doing something to deserve this treatment. These victims are isolated and usually suffer in silence. The media doesn't broadcast the pain and suffering of the victim. Some children will survive the bullies better than others, just like some adults survive being victimized. However, the injuries and the recovery depends largely on the number, frequency, severity and the duration of the bullying. Some children will leave school to escape the victimization. They might only be deprived of their education — to them, a small price to pay to escape the torment and humiliation. Some children will leave their hometowns to get away from the harassment and torture. Some children will turn to substance abuse and self-medicate in an attempt to escape their pain and suffering. Some will lose self-confidence and always believe that there must be something wrong with them — that they must deserve it, like everyone said. Some children must leave this world to escape the pain and torture of the bully.

In Japan, parents filed a 22 million yen damage suit against the Tokyo Metropolitan Government and parents of two alleged bullies, claiming their 13 year old son's suicide was caused by bullying. The parents also claimed the school principal and several teachers not only failed to intervene in the harassment, but also assisted the bullies in their activities. The boy hanged himself in a railway restroom and left a note naming two classmates responsible for his anguish. The boy had been forced to serve as messenger for the other two and repeatedly was buried by them in mock funerals.

Domestically, schools face a significant liability exposure for bullying. The parents of a ten year old San Francisco boy sued five bullies and the San Francisco School District for $351,000 for failing to enforce the child's right to attend a safe, secure and peaceful school. The victim alleged that the bullies punched and intimidated him every day during the fall of his elementary school term of 1985.

Other children will learn to accept the physical and or psychological injuries inflicted upon them — supposedly just for fun. They will go to the doctors and take the medications and accept the fact that life goes on and it isn't always fair. They won't question why it isn't fair they were not allowed to get a public education just because someone didn't like the way they dressed or acted.

When we don't accept that bullying is a real crime, a crime that is not always charged and convicted in a court of law, but one in which a bully is the judge, jury and executioner, we dismiss the very real injuries suffered by the victims. Although the psychological injuries and the extent can be varied, they are real injuries. Sometimes, the symptoms are internalized and sometimes they are externalized — sometimes both. In either case, bullying is a crime, according to the many victims.

Many teachers are concerned about bullying. Teachers agree that kids calling each other names and picking on each other many times leads to physical violence. The key is to stop it at the elementary grade level and reinforce the no bullying policy through high school. Strong measures and consistency are crucial to stopping this abusive behavior.

Bullying strips away a victim's feelings of safety, leaving the person feeling, at times, totally vulnerable. A girl who received telephone threats from a boy became frightened at night when tree branches brushed her window. She thought her tormentor was trying to break into her room. In such an extreme case, a solution is hard to come by.

Many other, less threatening, kinds of bullying can be handled in a constructive way, however.

Pellegrini and Bartini (2000) have suggested that aggression in the form of bullying is a strategy used by "low ranking individuals" when they enter a new social structure such as moving from elementary school to middle school. Their findings indicated that bullying behaviors increase at this point, and once dominance is established by an individual, aggressive behaviors tend to decline. Indeed, children making the transition to adolescence actually increase their use and endorsement of bullying behaviors (Crick and Werner, 1998).

When a landmark criminal trial in Victoria, B.C., of two 16 year old girls ended with a guilty verdict, another chapter was added to the saga of teen bullying that leads to murder and suicide. Along with Reena Virk, Hamed Nastoh and many others, the name of Dawn Marie Wesley, 14, was added to the list of casualties. Dawn Marie hanged herself. Her two former friends were charged after they were named in the suicide note she left behind in November 2000. The case, which centered on bullying, was the first time the province has brought schoolgirls into court after a suicide to face such charges. A youth court judge found one of them guilty of criminal harassment. The other was acquitted of uttering threats following an emotional trial attended by Dawn Marie's mother and the mothers of the two girls charged. During the trial in a Fraser Valley courtroom, the harsh reality of teen cold-heartedness, where bullying and threats sharply contrast with the idyllic and perhaps non-existent days of adolescent innocence, was on display. Youth court Judge Jill Rounthwaite indicated there was no doubting the threats of one teen were meant to intimidate Wesley, but felt the Crown failed to prove beyond a reasonable doubt the threats were made by a second teenaged girl. A spokesperson for the Attorney General in Victoria said under the Young Offenders Act, the maximum sentence from criminal harassment is six months in custody or 24 months probation (Joyce, 2000).

Whose Problem Is It?

It starts out young and it starts out small — a push during kindergarten recess or some under-the-breath name calling when first graders are lining up in the cafeteria. It's dubbed bullying or, to give it an update, harassment. Everybody knows it happens and, depending on which grade you are talking about and which survey you use, anywhere from eight percent to 25 percent of students say they are victimized by bullies at school. A far greater number say they have witnessed bullying (42 percent) or simply know it's happening in their school (56 percent).

It wasn't that long ago that schools took a kids-will-be-kids attitude and advised students to ignore the problem or even deemed the victim just as responsible as the bully. For a variety of reasons, that mode of operating doesn't work and probably never will. Statements from student assailants in the recent rash of school shootings in the United States lend credence to the assertion that persistent bullying leaves long-term scars on the victims.

So where and how does it all start? And, most importantly, how can teachers, principals and parents and all the other adults in children's lives play a role in stopping this age old problem? After the Littleton, Colorado, school massacre, opinions ran rampant on the best way to tackle the issue. For many teachers in the schools, the answer lies in smaller classes, more supportive parents, and a school climate that encourages staff and students to care about each other. Most importantly, training is needed — we need to evaluate what other school districts and communities are doing and adapt our own strategies.

Public schools do not intentionally teach violence or promote aggressive behavior in children. School violence is a community issue. Communities with higher rates of violence (domestic violence, assaults, etc.) report higher frequencies of school violence. If we accept this premise that schools are a reflection of their communities, then we must realize that schools alone cannot resolve the bullying issue. We need to promote the idea that there are multiple stakeholders, and we are all in this together. The current research predicts a bleak future for children who bully and for their victims unless there are corrective actions taken by those in a position to influence their lives. We must always remember that this work is targeted at specific behaviors, not specific individuals.

The epidemic of youth violence does not have a single or simple explanation and will not have a single or simple solution. The epidemic developed and evolved over several decades, so there are no quick fixes or magic solutions.

Chapter Four, Successful Interventions and Programs, will share several successful programs and campaigns for anti-bullying. Bullying is indeed a red flag indicating risk and the need for prevention and or intervention. The response to bullying must be part of a much larger effort.

Four

Successful Interventions and Programs

In America today, the little red schoolhouse is but a dream. In the real world of our nation, every two days the equivalent of a classroom of children is killed by firearms, in school or elsewhere. Homicide is the third leading cause of death for elementary and middle school children. In America, 50 million children walk through the doors of school each day. Twenty percent of high school students carried a weapon through those doors. Nationwide, one quarter of all suspensions from school were for violent incidents committed by elementary school students. Nearly one in four students and one in ten teachers say they have been victims of violence: on or near school property. From overt forms of physical violence to verbal violence such as threats and belittling comments, and to exclusion behaviors such as being left out on purpose, violence is common to all schools.

It is the more extreme forms of physical violence that capture the attention of both schools and communities while the less obvious forms of physical violence and non-physical violence are pretty much brushed off. The more frequent attacks that are less physically damaging are the most systematic and constant forms of violence in the school community. These non-physical or less physical attacks may be observed in the form of bullying, harassment, intimidation, racism, threats, assaults, or property damage, and often may be gender based.

Ochoa provides this example:

> Like other kids her age, Jamie Artman was bullied in middle school for no reason. One day, a group of boys picked her out of a crowd because she was wearing a necklace with a star pendant. "They started calling me

a witch, and they wouldn't leave me alone," said Artman, 14. "They just kept on pushing and pushing until they thought I would crack." But she didn't crack because she believed in herself and was part of a program called Students Taking A New Direction (STAND), which helps kids build self-esteem and confidence to conquer bullying.

Michigan through its new policy on bullying, is asking all school districts to develop their own plans to deal with the problem. The state Board of Education drafted its policy after increased incidents of school violence around the state and nation. Many of these incidents were the result of bullying, said Michael Warren, the board's secretary.

Even though 17 states have now passed anti-bullying legislation, the American schools are ten to fifteen years behind countries like Australia, Scandinavia, Great Britain and Japan.

One British headmaster whose school decided to launch an anti-bullying program said: "People could either say, 'That's a terrible school because they have bullying,' or they could say 'That's a good school because they are facing up to it,' we decided to take the risk" (website www.scre.ac.uk/bully/bullying.html).

——————— *What Parents Can Do* ———————

Parents have a first-hand view of what bullying can do to kids, and can be key catalysts in anti-bullying efforts. As one agonized parent relates, "My daughter has been bullied since she was at primary school. Daily she is called names like 'bitch' and 'slag.' We have tried everything but no-one listens. She has threatened to kill herself. All she wants is to be a happy kid at school with friends. I don't want any parent to suffer what we have suffered. I shall continue to fight" (website: www.scre.as.uk/bully/bullying.html).

I spoke with a parent who was allowing her child to enter public school for the first time. The child had previously been home schooled but the mother thought that during her middle and high school years her child should attend public schools. After two days of public school, the child refused to go back because of the bullying. The girls at the school were constantly taunting the child and wanting her to fight with them. The child was threatened because she talked to a boy that one of them liked. This particular child has never fought in her entire life and has led a very sheltered life. The girl was frightened to go to school.

Bullies and their behavior are a very real threat to our children today. The girls previously mentioned are not alone. As many as 58 percent of students skip school once or more because they were afraid of being picked on at school by a bully. The threat of violence is very real. Fists are one thing, but bullies are often armed with actual weapons. Bullying is not only a teen thing. Bullying is antisocial behavior that should not be permitted, in school or any where.

What to Do If Your Child Is a Victim

If your child is being bullied, listen to what they are saying and be supportive. It's important to make it clear that it's not their fault. Ask your child how they have been dealing with the bullying, and talk about what else can be done and what action you can both take to solve the problem. Reassure them you will consult them before taking action. Remember that it is very hard for the victim to solve the problem. Other people must make this happen for them. Give your child lots of support and encouragement. It takes a lot of courage to stand up to this type of abuse. At the same time, make sure your child understands that you do not expect them to handle the situation alone.

Discuss bullying with other parents or support groups who are able to suggest ways they have helped their own children. Talk to your child's school administrators and ask them what they can do to stop the bullying — suggest that the school contact the bully's parents or appoint an adult counselor to the bully. Encourage the school to develop a no-bullying policy if they don't already have one in place, and keep working with the school until the bullying stops. You can help your child develop a plan to deal with bullying, including how to get help. For example, help your child list all the adults they trust, whom they could talk to or go to for help. Write the names and telephone numbers on a card that they carry with them. Children should first try ignoring the bully, telling the bully to stop and walking away whenever the bully starts. Encourage your child to always tell an adult they can trust. Explain to your child this isn't tattling, they have a right to be safe. If your child is different in some way, help them to be proud of it; a confident child is less likely to be bullied and will also be better at dealing with the bully.

If your child is being bullied your first impulse might be to contact the bully's parent. When children are teased or tyrannized, the parental impulse is to grab the telephone and rant. However, bullying is on the rise and parental supervision on the decline, so calling moms and dads is more futile than ever. Such calls often lead to playground recriminations and don't really teach our children any lessons about how to navigate the world and resolve conflicts. Many parents are blown away by the idea that their child is being cruel. In a recent police department study in Oak Harbor, Washington, 89 percent of local high school students said they had engaged in bullying behavior. Yet only 18 percent of parents thought their children would act as bullies (Zaslow).

In a new national PTA survey, 25 percent of parents support contacting other parents to deal with bullying. But many educators warn that those conversations can be misinterpreted, causing tempers to flare. Instead, they say, parents should get objective outsiders, like teachers or administrators, to mediate (Zaslow).

Meanwhile, if you get a call from a parent who is angry about your child's bullying, listen without getting defensive.

If you feel you must call a parent, there are strategies. Keep in mind that parents view criticism of their children as criticism of their parenting. Rather than call their child a monster, say, "I'm worried about the relationship between our children." Be open-minded. Recess can often be 30 minutes of whispering, mimicking or sneering among children. Who started what? Perhaps your child is less innocent than he contends.

For a principal, it's very aggravating to call a parent when a child is being aggressive and having the parent respond that they have taught their children to take up for themselves. In other words, if someone hits you, you hit back. Also, parents tend to be on the offense when someone calls home to report aggressive incidents. Frequently, their response is "Did you see him do it?" or "What kind of punishment did the other kid get?" These responses from parents do not do anything to eliminate the aggressive behavior or eliminate the problem.

If your child is a victim of a bully, there are ways to deal with the problem:
- Teach your children at a young age to stay away from others who exhibit bullying behavior.
- Teach your children to be assertive but not aggressive when

approached by a bully. Tell them to walk away, and get help from an adult in dangerous situations.

- Teach your children never to use a gun or other weapon to defend themselves from bullies.
- Pay attention to symptoms that your child may be a victim of bullying, including withdrawal, sudden lack of interest in school, a drop in grades and signs of physical abuse. (Detailed descriptions of symptoms are included in Chapter Three.)
- Ask questions of teachers and administrators; inquire about school policies for handling incidents of bullying or harassment.
- If your child is bullied at school, tell school officials immediately. Keep written records of names, dates, times and circumstances of the incidents and give a copy to the principal.
- If school personnel make excuses for the bullying behavior, or refuse to address the incident, report the incident to the superintendent or the local board of education and demand the issue be addressed.
- Listen to your children. Encourage them to talk about school, other children in the class, and the walk or ride to and from school so you can identify any problems they are having.
- Take children's complaints of bullying seriously. Probing a seemingly minor complaint may uncover more severe grievances. Children are often afraid or ashamed to tell anyone that they have been bullied, so listen to their complaints.
- Work with other parents to ensure that the children in your neighborhood are supervised closely on their way to and from school.
- Don't bully your children yourself nor allow other family members. Use nonphysical, consistently enforced discipline measures as opposed to ridiculing, yelling at, or ignoring your children when they misbehave.
- Help children learn the social skills they need to make friends. A confident, resourceful child who has friends is less likely to be bullied or to bully others. Help them develop friendships. Stimulate your child to meet and interact with new peers. A new environment with new peers can provide a new chance for a victimized child.
- Motivate your child to participate in physical activities or sports.

Physical exercise can result in better physical coordination and less body anxiety. This, in turn, can increase your child's self-esteem and improve peer relations.

- Praise children's kindness toward others. Let children know that kindness is valued.
- Teach children ways to resolve arguments without violent words or actions. Teach children self-protection skills — how to walk confidently, stay alert to what's going on around them, and to stand up for themselves verbally.
- Provide opportunities for children to talk about bullying, perhaps when watching television together, reading aloud, playing a game, or going to the park or movie.
- Recognize that bullies may be acting out feelings of insecurity, anger, or loneliness. If your child is a bully, help get to the bottom of the problem. Seek out specific strategies you can use at home from a teacher, school counselor, or a child psychologist.

Parents might consider asking the school to implement a comprehensive anti-bullying program. A home and school association meeting to discuss and support such an initiative can be helpful.

If you suspect your child may be a victim of bullying, it's best to ask the question outright. Ask your child directly how he or she is spending their lunch time; or what it's like walking home or taking the school bus. Ask if there are any children at school who are bullies, without personalizing it. And then meet with teachers, ask how they deal with conflict when it occurs. If you are certain your child is being bullied, let the school know you take it seriously, and ask what can be done to help.

Some parents find it embarrassing to learn that their child is being bullied. But a few things to remember will make it easier to deal with:

- Be a good listener. Stay calm, and give your child plenty of time to tell you how he or she feels. Make it clear it's not your child's fault. Above all, don't suggest that your child simply fight back. That may increase your child's chances of further victimization. Some children are not aggressive by nature and you can't change that.
- Don't overreact. Ask yourself, is this serious enough to discuss with the teacher? With the principal? With the police?
- Help your child avoid the situations that expose him or her to

bullying. If it occurs on the way to or from school, find a safe route and arrange for an older child companion. Also, point out places the child can go for help. Finally, let the school authorities know if there is a problem, and keep a written record of incidents and who was involved.

What to Do If Your Child Is a Bully

What every parent doesn't want to hear — your child is behaving like a bully.

Your first response will probably be defensive. Disarm the situation and buy yourself some time to process what is being said. For example, "Instead of labeling my child, please tell me what happened." Make yourself really listen. Remember that this discussion is ultimately about the well-being of your child, regardless of how it is framed.

Parents are heavily involved in their children's lives and can see how they behave daily. That position denies them the right to claim ignorance. Part of parenting is actively listening. It's more difficult with teenagers, but that's a challenge, not an excuse. Noticing changes in appearances, habits and attitude are all part of monitoring and assessing whether intervention is needed, whether victimization or aggression is suspected.

Schools need parents to be their partners in preventing dangerous situations. Equally, parents need to trust that schools will respect and respond to their warnings and suspicions.

Even if your child is behaving aggressively or acting like a bully, remember that this behavior is probably coming from your child's feelings of vulnerability. You need to look for what is going on in your child's interactions with others and what is going on internally, causing your child to behave that way. Some suggestions for parents of bullies are:

- Teach your child to recognize and express emotions nonviolently.
- Teach conflict-management and conflict-resolution skills.
- Emphasize talking out the issue rather than hitting.
- Promote empathy by pointing out the consequences for others of the child's verbal and physical actions.
- Don't put down a bully. Bullies are intolerant of any insult to their self-concept.

- Model for your child the kind of behavior you want him or her to exhibit.
- Make clear to your child that you take bullying seriously, and will not tolerate such behavior in the future.
- Develop a consistent family rules system. Use praise and reinforcement for rule-following behavior. Use consistent, non-hostile, negative consequences for rule violation. Set a good example for your child by following the rules yourself. If your child observes aggressive behavior by you, he or she is more likely to act aggressively toward peers.
- Seek help from a mental health professional.

In talking with your child, do not blame. Do not get into a discussion about the whys of what happened. You should focus on several key points:

- Explain that bullying is not acceptable in your family or in your society.
- Remember to role-play or act out the new behaviors.
- If your child is feeling frustrated or angry or aggressive, "How can I help you with this? Who could you go to in school if you see yourself getting into this type of situation again?"
- Specify concretely the consequences if the aggression or bullying continues.

You want to stop this behavior, understand your child's feelings, then teach and reward more appropriate behavior.

How Do You Discourage a Child from Being a Bully?

Take a look at your parenting practices. We have an adult problem, not a youth problem. The hardest psychological and emotional bullying shows, no visible signs, no mercy, is easy to cover up ... but so long-lasting and debilitating. The examples set by so many people in supervisory positions are not examples of coaching and leading, but rather intimidating, bullying and threatening others.

Are you a bully at home? Do you frequently criticize your child or demand unquestioning obedience at every turn? Do you use spanking as a punishment? If so, you're sending a message to your child that anger, violence and intimidation are ways to get what you want. Very likely, your child will turn around and use similar tactics on peers.

Watch your tone — and your message. It's important for parents and caregivers to examine the tone of voice they use when speaking to children. Avoid undue criticism. Children learn by example, and someone who is belittled at home may resort to such tactics when dealing with peers.

Start to teach the art of negotiation early on. The preschool years are the time to begin to teach children to mediate their own disputes. If your toddler is wrestling a toy from the hands of a playmate, jump in and offer an alternative. With toddlers, parents and caregivers need to watch and intervene when trouble begins.

Don't be a wimp. Parents also produce a bully be being overly permissive. By giving in when a child is obnoxious or demanding, they send the message that bullying pays off. Children actually feel more secure when they know parents will set limits.

Parents and teachers need to take a hard-line approach to childhood aggression. Adults must make it clear that aggressive behavior in school, the neighborhood or at home is not acceptable and will not be tolerated. Children should be encouraged to report aggression and threats. Parents and school staff must deal with these incidents seriously.

When aggression is tolerated, everyone loses— the bullies, the victims and the bystanders. They are all learning that violence is acceptable and that is not the lesson we want to teach our children.

Bullying can be eliminated if adults and children become partners in this crusade against cruelty. Parents can play a role in reducing bullying. Research shows that the success of any program is 60 percent grounded in whether the same kinds of approaches are used at home (Labi, 2001).

If you discover your child is bullying other children, stay calm. Try to find out how and why they have been behaving this way. Explain to your child that bullying is wrong and try to get your child to understand what it's like for the victim. Ask how they would feel if someone was bullying them. Talk about what they think might help them to stop bullying and show them how to join on with other children without bullying them.

Praise them when they play or work cooperatively with other children without resorting to bullying. Talk to adults at your child's school, and find out if they have appropriate programs to help children who bully, or seek help from school counselors. In some cases, parents can help by controlling their own behavior and by making it clear that bullying is unacceptable.

——————— *What Schools Can Do* ———————

It is the National Education Association's top goal in launching a National Bullying Awareness Campaign to reduce and eventually eradicate bullying in our public schools. Convincing research indicates that this goal can best be achieved by fostering the active involvement of teachers, administrators, school support personnel, parents and community. Therefore, NEA is enlisting collaboration in this effort by other national and community organizations. Bullying and harassment are community issues that need multifaceted, systematic approaches which can include all community and national stakeholders. An early partner in this nationwide campaign has been the American Association of University Women. Other national organizations are expected to join in the near future.

The bullying problem in schools won't go away on its own. The reason is obvious: there are lots of bullies in the world, and lots of role models for children in their own homes or communities and in angry personalities they see in the media. We live in very confrontational times. Drivers rage at each other regardless of who is at fault. Television talk show participants scream at each other, gaining audience support by being louder and more aggressive.

Adult behavior is crucial to the success of any anti-bullying initiative. All adults in school must become aware of the extent of the bully-victim problems in their own school and community. These adults must then become engaged in a focused and sustained effort to change the situation. There exist a number of comprehensive bullying preventive programs which can help schools restructure the existing school environment to reduce opportunities and rewards for bullying behavior. These programs focus on creating a school climate of respect, acceptance and caring. Statewide promotion of proven anti-bullying programs which are supported with staff training and continuing assistance in implementation would be a powerful intervention toward diminishing the effects of bullying behavior.

Schools have a huge problem dealing with these young aggressors; parents have an even greater responsibility to be alert and to recognize if their own child is a bully or a victim.

Teachers and administrators cannot look away. In some cases of schoolyard bullying, some authority figure saw it happening and did not do anything about the situation. Students, too, do nothing even when they witness bullying. Under zero tolerance rules, they know the limits and are given the means to report bullying without being targeted as snitches.

A written anti-bullying policy distributed to everyone in the school community can help to send the message that bullying incidents will be taken seriously. To be effective, the policy must be fairly and consistently applied. Mapping a school's hot spots for bullying incidents can be very helpful. Once problematic locations have been pinpointed through survey responses or a review of disciplinary records, supervision can be concentrated where it is most needed. Providing better supervision is not necessarily costly. Principals can assign teachers and staff members to have supervisory duties in these areas. To achieve permanent changes in how students interact, negative consequences have to be provided and positive behavior through modeling, coaching, prompting, praise and other forms of reinforcement are necessary. Schools need to take a proactive role by implementing programs that teach students social skills, conflict resolution, anger management and character education.

Basic Principles for Prevention and Intervention

Any anti-bullying program will be more successful if educators:
- Strive for awareness and warm, positive involvement of adults, teachers, principals, counselors and parents.
- Set and stick to firm limits as to what behavior is unacceptable.
- Consistently apply non-hostile, non-physical consequences for rule violation and unacceptable behavior.
- Encourage adults to act as authorities and positive role models in students' academic learning and social relationships in school.

Creating a Whole-School Campaign

The school, or preferably the school district, can initiate a whole-school campaign. This involves strong commitment and a willingness to work together on the part of everyone involved. It must include all school personnel, other professionals as needed, students and parents. These elements are important to a successful campaign:

- A code of conduct, effectively communicated to all students.
- Making the school become a telling school. Any child who is bullied by another child or adult, or who sees another child being bullied, is urged to report the incident to designated school personnel.
- Coaching on what to do when being bullied and how to describe the incidents to adults, available to children in the early stages of the implementation of this program.
- Experts from outside the school for staff training. There are a number of good programs that can be brought into the school district to assist in the whole school campaign.
- Social skills instruction, incorporated into classroom activities and school events. Wise selection of materials can increase students' awareness of when they are being bullied and how to respond.
- Demonstration of alternative behavior shown to students exhibiting bullying behavior.
- A common vocabulary related to bullying as harassment and positive interpersonal relations. When the language used in bullying awareness activities becomes the language of the school, the incidents of bullying will diminish.

A constructive approach must be taken to minimize or avoid labeling children inappropriately and ensure that conclusions are not drawn prematurely, thereby risking inappropriate responses, interventions or disciplinary actions. Currently a tendency exists to blame children for problem behaviors rather than trying to understand what may be underlying their behavior. Environmental and social influences must be considered. What role does the media play? What kind of role modeling by parents, teachers and other adults promotes bullying or healthy social interaction? What is the relationship between bullying and exposure to family violence, which is well described and frequently occurring risk factor for involvement in violence?

School Level Interventions

School level interventions are designed to improve school climate. These interventions target the entire school population and include:

- Establishing a bullying prevention coordinating committee. This committee will coordinate all aspects of a school's violence prevention efforts, including anti-bullying.
- Administering an anonymous questionnaire survey. A student questionnaire can determine the nature and extent of bully-victim problems in the school.
- Holding a school conference day. Raise school and community awareness and involvement by creating a long term anti-bullying plan. In addition to school personnel, selected students and parents should participate.
- Improving supervision and outdoor environment. Provide an adequate number of adults to supervise recess, lunch and breaks in an effort to intervene quickly in student conflicts.
- Involving parents. Conduct meetings with and disseminate information to parents at the school to make them aware of the school's anti-bullying plan of action.

Classroom Level Interventions

Classroom level interventions are designed to improve an individual classroom's social climate. These interventions target the entire class and include:

- Establishing classroom rules against bullying. Involve students in creating rules against bullying in order to develop a student's personal responsibility for conforming to those rules.
- Creating positive and negative consequences of behavior. Establish social reinforcement for positive behavior and sanctions for undesirable behavior. The negative consequence should cause discomfort without being perceived as malicious or unfair. Negative consequences should be appropriate and related to the behavior. Extra assignments, such as homework or copying from a dictionary, should not be used.
- Holding regular classroom meetings. Provide a forum for teachers and students to develop, clarify and evaluate rules for anti-bullying behavior.
- Meeting with parents. Hold general classroom or grade level meetings with parents to improve school family communication and keep parents informed about anti-bullying efforts.

Individual Level Interventions

Classroom level interventions are designed to change or improve the behavior of students in general. These interventions target specific students who are involved in bullying, either as bullies or victims. A person in authority should talk to the bully or bullies immediately after they have behaved inappropriately. These talks should include:

- Documenting involvement of participation in bullying,
- Sending a clear, strong message that bullying is not acceptable,
- Warning the child or children that future behavior will be closely monitored, and
- Warning that additional negative consequences will be administered if bullying does not stop.

Serious talks with the victim and his or her parents should occur after a bullying incident. These talks should include:

- Documenting specific bullying incidents that include: How did the bullying start? What happened? How did it end? Who participated and in what way?
- Providing the victim information about the teacher's plan of action in dealing with the bully or bullies, and
- Attempting to persuade the victim to immediately report any new bullying episodes or attempts to the teacher.

When a bullying situation is discovered, the teacher should contact the parents concerned. Depending on the situation, meetings can be held together with the parents of both the bully and the victim, or to minimize tension, meetings can be held with each family separately. A teacher might want to invite the school psychologist, guidance counselor, principal or assistant principal to attend.

If anti-bullying measures are in place and the problem persists despite these measures, moving the aggressive student can bring about change. If possible, the aggressive student should be moved before considering moving the victim. This solution should not be taken lightly, and all concerned parents and teachers should plan and consult with each other.

Dealing with Bullying Incidents

Each school board or district has its own policies and procedures for dealing with discipline and violent incidents at school. These poli-

cies and procedures should be reviewed at the start of each school year
in order to see if you have set procedures and policies for bullying
behaviors. Suggested steps for intervening in bullying situations
include:

- Intervene immediately: stop the bullying behavior as soon as
  you see it or become aware of it.
- Talk to the bully and talk to the victim separately. If more than
  one child is involved in perpetrating the bullying, talk to each
  perpetrator separately, in quick succession.
- If a peer mediation program is in place, be very careful in refer-
  ring cases where there is bullying, as the power imbalance will
  likely make this a very intimidating situation for the victim. The
  victim's communication and assertiveness skills may be very
  low, and will be further eroded by the fear resulting from past
  intimidation and fear of future retaliation. You may wish to
  exclude such cases from peer mediation.
- Consult with administrator and other teachers, as well as staff,
  to get a wider reading on the problem and to alert them to the
  problem. Get advice as to how this situation fits with school
  policies.
- Expect that the perpetrator will deny his or her actions or responsibilities. Refer to class and school codes in telling the bully why
  their behavior was unacceptable. Tell them what behavior you
  expect of them. Inform the bullies of the sanctions which will
  be imposed and that their parents will be involved.
- Reassure the victim that all possible steps will be taken to prevent a recurrence.
- Inform the bully's parents of as soon as possible. A quick call to
  the home the same day is preferable, followed by an appointment at school for parents, if it is deemed necessary. Better
  results are obtained when parents are involved early in a bullying situation, before behavior patterns are entrenched and
  extremely serious.
- Involve parents in designing a creative plan of action, whenever
  possible.
- For victims, it is important to involve them in groups and situations where they can make appropriate friends and develop
  their social skills and confidence. An example of this is a peer

support group, new student orientation group, a co-operative learning group in class, or a special activity group or club. Parents can also arrange for these kinds of opportunities outside of the school.

- For the bullies, specific re-education as to their behavior is important, in addition to sanctions such as removal of privileges, detention, etc. Some schools have had success with in school detention where aggressive students must complete social skill modules designed to reduce aggressive behavior and develop empathy for others.

- Follow up in communicating with parents and with other teachers and administrators about the situation until it is clearly resolved.

- Monitor the behavior of the bully and the safety of the victim on a schoolwide basis.

- If the bully will not change his or her behavior despite concerted efforts on the part of the school, he or she should be removed form the class or school, or transferred to an alternative program. Consequences for the perpetrators will be of considerable interest to all students and will set the tone for future situations.

Steps to a Successful Schoolwide Program

Bullying is a problem that occurs in the social environment as a whole. The bullies' aggression occurs in social contexts in which teachers and parents are generally unaware of the extent of the problem and other children are either reluctant to get involved or simply do not know how to get help. Given this situation, effective interventions must involve the entire school community rather than focus on the perpetrators and victims alone. There is a need to develop whole-school bullying policies, implement curricular measures, improve the schoolground environment and empower students through conflict resolution, peer counseling, and assertiveness training. An approach that involves interventions at the school, class and individual levels must include the following components:

- An initial questionnaire can be distributed to students and adults. The questionnaire helps both adults and students to become aware of the extent of the problem, helps to justify intervention efforts, and serves as a benchmark to measure the impact of improvements in school climate once other intervention components are in place.

- A parental awareness campaign can be conducted during parent-teacher conference days, through newsletters, and at P.T.A. meetings. The goal is to increase parental awareness of the problem, point out the importance of parental involvement for program success, and encourage parental support of program goals. Questionnaire results are publicized.
- Teachers can work with students at the class level to develop rules against bullying. Many programs engage students in a series of formal role-playing exercises and related assignments that can teach those students directly involved in bullying alternative methods of interaction. These programs can also show other students how they can assist victims and how everyone can work together to create a school climate where bullying is not tolerated.
- Other components of anti-bullying programs include individualized interventions with the bullies and victims, the implementation of cooperative learning activities to reduce social isolation, and increasing adult supervision at key times.

In the school setting, children experience bullying as a frequent challenge. It is important to counter views that bullying is an inevitable part of school life. The wider community, and particularly the adults within it, must take responsibility for making it clear that bullying is an act of violence and will not be tolerated in our society. Schools have an obligation to ensure they are a safe place for all students. Any meaningful response to bullying must recognize that a whole community approach is necessary. Such whole group approach may involve:

- increasing staff knowledge and awareness of bullying issues;
- gathering information about the current situation and the school's strategies;
- developing a common understanding of bullying within the school;
- consultation with parents, community groups, and students, to develop an anti-bullying program;
- development of advice and information pamphlets and dissemination; and

- intervening in ways that do not model the actions that are unacceptable (punishment, blaming, excluding).

At Central York Middle School in Pennsylvania, all students sign anti-teasing pledges and are taught to appropriately manage their anger. Since this practice was started, the school reports a reduction in fistfights. At Laurel Elementary in Fort Collins, Colorado, students undergo "Be Cool" training in which counselors present them with provocative situations and help them recognize the difference between a "hot response" and a "cool response." To discourage peers from acting as an audience to bullying behavior, Seeds University Elementary School in Los Angeles has a policy of sending bystanders as well as bullies to after school mediation. Students and their parents sign a contract at the beginning of the school year acknowledging they understand it is unacceptable to ridicule, taunt, or attempt to hurt other students. If an incident occurs, it can be used as an opportunity to educate students about alternative ways of resolving similar situations in the future.

What Students Can Do

At the center of any approach to bullying prevention are those individuals most directly affected by and responsible for bully-victim situations—the students in the school. Most students are neither bully nor victim. They are, however, witnesses to the bullying that takes place around them. Students can promote a positive school climate by discouraging bullying behavior among their peers, promoting inclusion of all others in their activities and seeking to foster acceptance of differences.

Students need to be educated so they will know what to do and how to diffuse a bullying situation. Students might want to do the following when encountered by a bully:

- Stand straight and tall and look him straight in the eye.
- Be polite, but firm. Tell the bully, "Stop it, I don't like it. Leave me alone."
- If at all possible, don't cry or show you are upset. Walk away if you can't hide your feelings.
- Report incidents to an adult you trust. Expect action to be taken.

What Brothers, Sisters and Friends Can Do

Brothers, sisters and friends often know long before the teacher does if someone is being bullied. Sometimes the person being bullied asks them not to do anything. Sometimes they do nothing in case the bullies start to pick on them.

But doing nothing usually means that the bullying carries on, or the bullies become more confident and choose more victims. Part of the fun that bullies get comes from the reaction of bystanders. If you do nothing, bullies may think you approve of what they are doing. Siblings and friends might want to:

- Persuade the person being bullied to talk to an adult — this may be a teacher or a parent.
- Encourage the person being bullied to talk to you about what is happening.
- Offer to speak to an adult on the bullied person's behalf.
- Let the bullies know that you are not frightened of them and that you are determined to see that they stop.
- Raise the issue of bullying with the student council (if your school has one) or in classroom discussions.
- Involve as many people as possible. In particular, try to make sure that teachers know what is going on — but, most of all, talk to someone.

Siblings and friends should not do the following:

- Do not use violence against the bullies— you may end up being accused of being a bully.
- Do not tell the person being bullied to deal with the problem on their own — if they could, they wouldn't need your help.
- Do not try to deal with things on your own.

The key messages to get across to someone being bullied are:

- It's not your fault that you are being bullied
- You don't have to face this on your own.

What Communities Can Do

Bullying and harassment are community issues and require total community involvement to find solutions. Numerous opportunities

will arise from community involvement. A community task force could
do the following:

- Develop a multifaceted, systematic approach that includes all
  community stakeholders.
- Sponsor a conference or forum to educate and raise awareness.
- Create a speaker's bureau to speak on the issue.
- Encourage civic groups to provide venues for presentations.
- Work with the mayor's office to celebrate "Respect for Every-
  one" campaigns.
- Sponsor "Teach-Ins" for parents and community using students,
  parents and teachers to discuss strategies to prevent bullying.
- Partner with higher education institutions to publish data show-
  ing how bullying contributes to absenteeism and low achieve-
  ment in school.
- Connect with service learning programs in schools.
- Arrange for public relations support from local television sta-
  tions, radio and newspaper.
- Sponsor early childhood and after school programs.
- Schedule business roundtable discussions.

Community resources need to be made available to the families
of children who bully, in order to help them develop a home environment characterized by warmth, positive interest, and involvement by
adults. Schools, homes and communities need to be places where there
are firm parameters established and negative consequences are consistently applied in cases of violations of rules and other unacceptable
behaviors, and where adults act as authorities and positive role models. Access to school based mental health services would be very
beneficial to the families of children who bully. Communities need to
strive to provide resources to meet all of the diverse needs of our youth.

The medical community recognizes bullying as a serious public
health issue. At its own expense, the Washington State Medical Association distributes a brochure to pediatricians and family physicians
statewide. Doctors will soon give it to parents of school age children
during examinations. Further, doctors will discuss bullying with parents and children as part of every checkup. The partnership with the
medical community is recognition of the seriousness of this issue to
the health of our children, and is part of the Attorney General Office's
ongoing work to help reduce youth violence in Washington.

------ *Examples of Effective Programs* ------

"Peaceful Schools" is a booklet published by the Northwestern Regional Educational Laboratory (located in Alaska, Idaho, Montana, Oregon and Wasington). It calls for schools to address the following issues in preventing bullying:

- The physical plant should feel safe to students and staff; entrances should be visible, hallways well lighted and playgrounds monitored.
- A strong sense of organization tends to permeate safe schools.
- Safe schools discipline students for disruptive behavior early and fairly. For students to feel safe, discipline needs to be fair, consistent, and clear. Rules and guidelines need to be clearly and repeatedly communicated to students and parents.
- Schools must challenge social norms that encourage violence.
- Advance planning is needed for a timely response in the event of a crisis.
- In-service training for teachers helps them understand a violence-prevention curriculum.

The Northwest Regional Educational Laboratory has been selected to operate the National Safe Schools Resource Center to provide training and technical assistance to the nation's schools and communities to assist them in creating crime and violence free learning environments.

Practice Playground. Riverside Elementary in Waterford, Michigan, tells their students to report all incidents of inappropriate behavior to the teachers. Then the teacher, victim and bully go to a classroom planning center to discuss the problem. Later, the bully attends "Practice Playground" which has constant adult supervision in small group settings, far away from the larger recess group. The purpose is to teach appropriate social skills. Children misbehave for attention, control or fun. This program identifies what is missing for the child. Children have few coping skills and they've been trained not to tattle, and adults are in a quandary about how to respond.

School-Based-Anti-Violence Program (ASAP). This is a program with special focus on gender issues in violence and violence in intimate relationships. It was developed by the London (Ontario) Family

Court Clinic in conjunction with London educators and community members. Support is provided through a collaborative, broadly based partnership of community groups and agencies.

Specific goals include:

- Providing knowledge about the incidence and causes of family and dating violence;
- Shaping more pro-social attitudes in family and dating relationships;
- Offering knowledge of community agency resources for people affected by violence; and
- Generating ideas by students to ameliorate problems of violence, e.g., physical, sexual and verbal abuse; violence in the media and sports.

Major program activities include:

- The development of administration-based and school-based planning committees;
- Information presentations and workshops;
- Special productions followed by in-class discussions;
- School-based action plans developed by students; and
- On-site counseling and referral services for students.

AASP is being implemented in sites across Canada.

Olweus Norwegian Anti-Bullying Program. This nationwide school-based violence prevention program focuses on strengthening sanctions against bullying behavior and supporting social norms for inclusive and pro-social behavior.

The program is based on an analysis of research on bully and victim characteristics. Bullies were generally confident and, if boys, tended to be physically stronger than others their age; they were not found to have underlying self-esteem or anxiety problems. Bullies tend to come from families where violence was condoned or modeled and where there were low levels of parental supervision. Victims were found to be anxious, socially isolated and lacking in confidence in their abilities and tended not to react assertively to aggression.

Major program activities include:

- Developing awareness of bullying;
- Involving adults in activities;
- Surveying bully-victim problems;
- Holding school conference days/class meetings about bullying;

- Providing better supervision during recess and lunch;
- Setting specific rules against bullying and implementing consistent and immediate consequences for aggressive behaviors;
- Conducting serious talks with bullies, victims and parents; and
- Initiating parent-teacher meetings on the topic.

An extensive and large scale evaluation showed a 50 percent reduction of self-reported victimization over a three year period, a reduction in anti-social behaviors such as vandalism and an improvement in the social climate in schools. Teachers viewed the program as realistic and beneficial.

Common Sense Solutions. In July 2000, Washington state Attorney General Christine Gregoire initiated a task force of professionals who explored the pervasiveness of bullying, the seeds of violence that harassment and intimidation can plant in schools, the impacts of bullying on children and ways to reduce the problem. The task force worked countless hours in research, brainstorming and discussion. Members agreed that it was time to act on the issue and decided to pursue legislation as the first step. The anti-bullying bill supported by the Attorney General proposed to:

- Require that school districts ban bullying, harassment and intimidation. Schools would be required to notify students of the policy. Further, the bill would require districts to incorporate information and the anti-bullying policy into their existing faculty training programs.
- Require school districts to discuss the policy with students and train all school employees and volunteers who have significant contact with students.
- Encourage schools and school districts to form bullying prevention task forces, programs, and other initiatives that involve school staff, students, administrators, volunteers, parents, law enforcement and community members.
- Reinforce that students and school staff have a right to report bullying without fear of retaliation.
- Encourage employees who witness bullying to report it to the proper authorities, and grant them civil immunity from damages if they make such reports promptly.

There is no single answer to the problem of bullying. Legislation alone will not stop every bully from physically or verbally tormenting a peer. However, this Common Sense Solutions legislation is an important first step toward bringing bullying out of the shadows of school hallways and playgrounds and establishing its prominence as a threat to the safety of our children.

Take a Stand. This is revolutionary approach to prevention of bullying. Starting with kindergarten and progressing through fifth grade, children learn about bullying, its effects, how to stop it and the importance of mutual acceptance and respect. The program fosters acceptance from the earliest age possible that bullying will not take place, creating a new standard for interpersonal relationships. Just as children led the drive to use seatbelts and to reduce smoking, they are the leaders in setting a new course for how we treat one another. The Take A Stand Program creates a schoolwide community of interpersonal problem solving and mutual respect that has been embraced by school administrators, teachers, parents and children. The program was created by Dr. Sherryll, who specializes in youth at risk. She is internationally recognized for her preventive programs and creating models for maximizing community wide participation in prevention effectiveness.

Steps to Respect: A Bullying Preventive Program. This program was developed by the Committee for Children and designed to help schools decrease bullying and create a safe and respectful learning climate. It is a proactive, systematic approach for elementary schools to deal with bullying behavior. The program's broad scope is unique — it includes an extensive program guide (which includes research on bullying and detailed, step-by-step implementation guidelines), teacher and staff training materials, multi-media lessons for children and a 90 minute parent overview session. A school can use these tools to help implement an effective anti-bullying campaign. The program is designed to rally an entire school community — students, staff, teachers and parents— against bullying. William King Elementary, a Nova Scotia (Canada) elementary school that piloted the program, saw an increase in children's reports of bullying after they started the program. Steps to Respect gives children a box of tools, skill steps they can use when confronted with bullying. A counselor at Assumption St. Bridget, a private Seattle school that also piloted the program, saw similar results and stated that students were no longer afraid to talk about what was going on in school.

No Bullying. This Johnson Institute (Minneapolis) curriculum, first implemented during the 1996–97 school year in schools across the country, describes the tell-or-tattle dilemma facing many victims of bullying. Teachers are given step-by-step guidelines on how to teach students the difference between telling and tattling. Teachers are also shown how to establish and use immediate consequences when dealing with bullies.

Bullyproof: A Teacher's Guide on Teasing and Bullying for Use with Fourth and fifth Grade Students. This guide by Lisa Sjostrom and Nan Stein contains 11 sequential lessons designed to help children understand the difference between teasing and bullying and to gain awareness about bullying and harassment through class discussions, role-playing, and writing, reading and art exercises.

Bully-Proofing Your School. This program, available from Sopris West, uses a comprehensive approach. Key elements include conflict resolution training for all staff members, social skills building for victims, positive leadership skills training for bullies, intervention techniques for those who neither bully nor are bullied, and the development of parental support.

Quit It! A Teacher's Guide on Teasing and Bullying. This guide by Merle Frosche, Barbara Sprung, and Nancy Mullin-Rinder with Nan Stein contains ten lessons. Each lesson is divided into activities geared to the developmental needs of students in kindergarten through third grade. Class discussions, role plays, creative drawing and writing activities, physical games and exercises and connections to children's literature give children a vocabulary and conceptual framework that allows them to understand the distinction between teasing and bullying.

Second Step, The Committee for Children. This curriculum teaches positive social skills to children and families, including skill building in empathy, impulse control, problem solving and anger management. Initial evaluations of Second Step indicate that second and third grade students engaged in more prosocial behavior and decreased physically aggressive behavior after participating in the program.

Charleston, South Carolina. In collaboration with the Medical University of South Carolina, staff at Alice Birney Middle School launched a unique violence prevention initiative that combines two model programs targeted at aggressive behavior; a comprehensive bullying prevention effort and multisystematic therapy for children with serious behavior problems. Following the bullying model intervention activities developed by Olweus (1993), the entire school participated in violence prevention activities to reduce bullying among the school's sixth, seventh and eighth graders. Activities included the development of rules against bullying, increased supervision on the playground, recess and lunch, role playing, discussions and other classroom activities and the active involvement of parents and community members. In addition, students who exhibit particularly aggressive behavior are invited to participate in multisystematic therapy (MST), an intensive family and home-based treatment that attempts to change how youth function in their natural settings—home, school and neighborhood. MST therapists have small caseloads (four to six families) and provide services in the family's home or at school. A therapist is available 24 hours a day, seven days a week.

Bully-Proofing Your School Program. Willow Creek Elementary School in suburban Englewood, Colorado, employed this program to increase the knowledge of staff and students, clear misconceptions regarding bullying, and emphasize the importance of a consistent schoolwide intervention. Staff were taught different methods for dealing with bullies and victims. Students were taught protective skills that gave them a sense of empowerment in dealing with bullying situations. The students were also encouraged to form a caring community in which everyone looks out for and sticks up for everyone else. During the first year, students in grades one through five participated in nine weeks of group meetings. Children also participated in optional sessions dealing with conflict resolution and diversity. Follow-up review sessions were conducted one to two months later. Kindergarten students were introduced to an abbreviated version of the program.

During the second year, first grade students were provided the entire program and students in grades two through five participated in a three-session review of the program. A series of student and parent surveys were conducted over the two year period. Based on these reports, the bully-proofing program appears to be impacting the school environment in a positive way. Central to the success of the program is the caring majority concept, whereby 80 percent of children who are neither bullies or victims set the climate for the school by working together to stop bullying. Perceptions of safety increased before the actual incidence of bullying declined.

Respect and Protect. Caruthersville Middle School in Missouri uses a violence prevention and intervention program developed by the Johnson Institute of Minneapolis. The program emphasizes a comprehensive approach to violence prevention, encouraging all school personnel to commit to a violence prevention plan and to consistently enforce measures to intervene when violent acts occur. School staff have learned to recognize and control actions that enable violence — actions such as denying, rationalizing, justifying, avoiding or blaming. They have also learned that appropriate consequences coupled with prevention and intervention programs will change negative behaviors and ultimately the school environment. Students are reminded daily that no form violence — including hurtful words, looks, signs or acts that cause harm to a person's body, feelings or possessions — will be tolerated. Students who engage in physical violence, bullying or intimidation are required to attend after-school violence intervention counseling that focuses on anger management and conflict resolution. Failure to attend results in suspension. Prevention programs that have been implemented at Caruthersville Middle School as part of its comprehensive approach include the Fight Free School program, Violence is Preventable exploratory course, the No Bullying program and Resolve All Problems Peacefully peer mediation program. The initial results of Respect and Protect look very positive. Results indicate a 16 percent reduction in the first year and a 25 percent reduction in the second year in the number of students involved in physical confrontations. Students are realizing they are responsible for their own behavior and if they choose to engage in unacceptable behavior, appropriate consequences will apply.

Coolien Challenge. This is an educational computer game; it uses interactive strategies for students to learn constructive problem solving skills. The main character enlists the aid of students to help settle 11 problems in a peaceful and effective way. A list of program resources is available from the National School Safety Center.

The **Arlington (Virginia) High School Continuation Program** links adult mentors with youth who have been involved in previous delinquent behavior.

Big Brother/Big Sisters of Martinville (Louisiana) provides weekly afternoon mentoring and activities such as sports and tutoring for at-risk youth.

SOS — Students Out Front. Canton Middle School in Canton, North Carolina, received a federal grant to establish an after school program for latch key students. Activities are created for those students who are at-risk and have been referred by teachers and staff. They have a coordinator who arranges tutoring, conflict resolution and mediation and have actively worked on bullying and conflict resolution. Reported incidents of bullying have decreased by 50 percent. The program currently has 35 students participating. They offer parent dinners with a program. Parent programs have included: adult education, technology, working with your child, mediation and role modeling. The after-school students go on field trips which have included hockey games, soccer, and the cultural arts. An additional item of the program includes an artist in residence who is teaching banjo lessons. For students to be eligible to participate in the program, they have to be in school and cannot be in in-school or out-of-school suspension. The SOS program is committed to providing experiences and opportunities for the academic and social success of the students. The program was endorsed and supported by many community groups and agencies. They have committed time and personnel for current programs as well as developing new programs. Cash and in-kind resources for this program have been committed by the Haywood County Schools with the use of the facility, the Literacy Council, which will provide training for volunteers, and others. Objectives include:

- reduce school suspension by 20 percent,
- expand personal growth in 50 percent of participants in year one,
- reduce contact with the juvenile justice among participants,
- build healthier self-esteem and positive growth by 35 percent, and
- improve academic performance of 75 percent of participants in reading and math.

After Hours. Waynesville Middle School and Central Elementary School in Waynesville, North Carolina, received a 21st Century Grant. This three year grant focuses on serving quality after-school programs and weekend and summer programs for pre-kindergarten through eighth graders. They offer a summer camp for middle school students and actually made a video entitled *Fear Factor*. The purpose of the video was to help elementary students make the transition to middle school. The video has received both state and national recognition. A Kinder Kamp was established for four year olds. The purpose of the program is to make the community a better place for young people during their out of school time. A family learning center has been established at both sites. After Hours is dedicated to offering more positive opportunities and fun activities for students. The program draws from comprehensive youth development models such as that of Michael Carrera (developed model on adolescent sexual health). Carrera's model has a ten year track record of success and shows that youth who are involved in a cluster of activities that provide them with encouragement, academic support, community service opportunities, and life or job skills make better decisions about bullying, drugs, alcohol and sexual activity. Youth who participate in school receive better job opportunities and look forward to a brighter future. After Hours strives to provide these developmental activities for youth in an environment which nurtures self-esteem, helps to deal with peer pressure and conflict, and encourages setting goals for the future. After Hours is continually developing a variety of activities. These activities center on tutoring, mentoring, leadership, environmental stewardship, government issues, media, volunteering, field trips, art, drama, cooking and nutrition, photography and music and dance. All activities are designed to build character, enhance academic performance, broaden experiences, and teach skills for living in harmony and life skills.

Red Deer Public Schools, Central Alberta, Canada, is a district where bullying is on the decline. The district's anti-bullying survey showed fewer students were bullied or threatened and fewer witnessed such behavior. There was an eight percent increase in the number of students who were never bullied or threatened at school compared to the district's previous survey. The number of students bullied or threatened a lot was reduced by one percent, dropping from five to four percent. There were several anti-bullying initiatives undertaken in schools. The biggest cause for the reduction was that students were less tolerant of bullying and were less likely to endure their friends being bullied or harassed. One successful intervention was talking to adults when bullying was taking place and allowing adults to handle the situation.

Students Against Bullying. McCormick Middle School in McCormick, South Carolina, because of high concern about incidents of bullying, instituted an anti-bullying program. The students named the program. Start up activities included staff meetings and in-service training for all teachers; establishment of a steering committee, including teachers and counselors; and involvement of parents through committee membership and communications that are sent home. For two years the activities were intense. Student training sessions occurred every two weeks, and administrative policy changes to support changed student behavior were adopted frequently. As an outgrowth of the anti-bullying focus, character education, conflict education and a mediation program are now in place. All students are involved in these activities. The aspects of the program that focused solely on bullying are less intense, but follow-up on the original program continues. The school has very strict rules regarding students showing respect to each other by not touching each other inappropriately. Students have cut much of the shoving, pushing and bullying behavior of the past. Statistics show bullying incidents have been reduced by 22 percent.

Jamison High School in Penrith, Australia, has been implementing a comprehensive whole-school program to tackle the problem of bullying in the school community. Their highly innovative approaches to this seemingly intractable social problem have been recognized nationally by their being awarded an Australian Violence Prevention Award, a joint Commonwealth-State initiative. Jamison High School's anti-bullying program includes:

- A clear and detailed anti-bullying policy which includes how the school will deal with bullying instances, as well as preventive strategies. This policy is included in the students handbook and distributed to all parents. Staff are regularly updated.
- The use of the Pikas Method of Share Concern as part of a highly articulated process for dealing with bullying instances.
- A student anti-bullying committee.
- Peer helpers.
- Student Welcomers to assist new students in settling into Jamison High School.
- Curriculum programming of anti-bullying in the PD/Health/PE and English/Drama subject areas.
- Peer support anti-bullying sessions for the upcoming year.
- A school publicity campaign for the community, staff and students.

Bully Proofing Your School. The Laramie School District in Cheyenne, Wyoming, uses this program, which includes training the school staff. This anti-bullying program has been implemented in several schools in the district. The program consists of a no-nonsense approach to ending bullying. This is accomplished through the enforcement of a zero-tolerance policy, training staff to intervene effectively and teaching students what they can do when bullying occurs. An important component of the program is the development of a caring community so that all students can intervene to stop bullies from abusing others. Parents are encouraged to learn about the program so they can collaborate with the school in reducing the problem. Students are taught to use the following strategies when challenged by bullies:

- **Help** — How to give or get it.
- **Assert** — How to stop someone from making fun of me without further provoking the bully.
- **Humor** — How to turn a jab into a joke — "Yeah, my glasses are so funny, they make me laugh too."
- **Avoid** — How to walk away.
- **Self-talk** — "I'm not stupid, I made an A on my project."
- **Own it** — "You're right, my hair's red but everyone in my family has red hair."

In a continuing effort to improve education for all students, bully-proofing schools will help teachers teach better by ridding the classroom of bullying disruptions. However, without adult intervention, bully problems will not go away.

Kindness Is Contagious uses cognitive-behavioral methods to decrease acts of peer abuse and school violence, increase acts of kindness and foster appropriate interpersonal skills in children K-12. As part of this comprehensive peer abuse prevention program, the STOP Violence Coalition provides schools, parent groups and youth agencies with training, curriculum materials and other resources to help create safe school environments where students can concentrate on learning. Each year over 10,000 educators, parents and students are trained in how to define and identify bullying and other inappropriate peer abuse behaviors.

Kia Kaha is a whole-school approach to eliminating bullying. It aims to help schools create environments where everyone feels safe, respected and valued and where bullying cannot flourish. This intervention program consists of a working booklet which gives a step-by-step guide to putting the whole-school approach in place, and five curriculum programs, one for each level of primary and secondary schools. This program was developed by the Youth Education Services (YES) of the New Zealand Police, working in close association with Specialist Education Services. The Crime Prevention Unit provided support and financial assistance. The general objectives of Kia Kaha are:

- Students, parents, caregivers and teachers recognize that bullying and harassment are unacceptable and will take steps to see that they do not occur in their school.
- Students, parents, caregivers and teachers will work together to create a safe learning environment based on mutual respect, tolerance and a respect for diversity.

Approximately 145 police education officers work full time in schools nationally, to deliver the YES programs in partnership with teachers. In Kia Kaha their role is to:

- Respond to inquiries from schools.
- Advise schools of the availability of the Kia Kaha program.
- Take part in an initial meeting where the principal finds out more about the program.
- Supply the initial inspection kit and provide the necessary Kia Kaha materials once the school decides to proceed.
- Assist the coordinator with the implementation of the whole-school approach.
- Plan the teaching program with teachers.
- Teach in partnership with teachers, to the extent decided at the local level.
- Take part in program evaluation.
- Maintain records of local school involvement.

The **Expect Respect** (1999) Program uses a preventive model that addresses social acceptance of bullying among students, teachers, and school staff. Its primary purpose is to improve peer relationships and communication skills among students. It attempts to help bullies understand the boundaries between appropriate and inappropriate behavior and teaches skills for responding to such behavior. After the first year of the program, a review of the evaluation findings indicated that a better understanding of the children's own definitions of bullying and teasing behaviors would help improve the curriculum. The program was implemented in six elementary schools in Austin, Texas. Elementary schools were chosen because research suggested interpersonal violence is learned behavior that can be prevented through education and early intervention. Without such early intervention, elementary school bullying has been shown to be predictive of more serious violent acts by individuals during later years. The Expect

Respect project was taught by trained facilitators once a week for 12 weeks throughout the semester and used curriculum developed by Nan Stein, Senior Research Scientist for the Center for Research on Women at Wellesley College (Mass.). The curriculum included core lessons of writing activities, reading assignments, class discussions, role plays, case studies, and homework assignments. In pilots of this lesson plan, children gained a conceptual framework and a common vocabulary that allowed them to find the distinctions between appropriate and inappropriate or playful and hurtful behavior. The program helped to reduce the extent of inappropriate behavior at intervention schools.

Best Aggression-Prevention Programs in Schools. In one of the first studies to compare existing school-based aggression prevention programs across the nation, researchers from the Children's Hospital of Philadelphia found that targeting programs to kindergarten and young elementary school students, focusing on aggression in girls as well as boys, and conducting programs in naturalistic settings like playgrounds are key factors in the success of aggression prevention in schools. By defining aggression broadly to include both physical aggression and relational aggression (gossiping, threatening to exclude from the peer group), effective aggression prevention programs are better able to target both boys and girls and focus on the everyday acts of aggression that occur on school playgrounds and that can lead to more serious violence in later years. The Children's Hospital Research team offers the following suggestions for designing and evaluating successful aggression prevention programs:

- Define aggression broadly;
- Focus on prevention and early intervention;
- Target young girls;
- Be culturally sensitive and foster collaboration between schools, families, and communities;
- Emphasize positive social behavior;
- Incorporate a strong research component;
- Conduct programs in naturalistic settings, such as on the playground; and
- Evaluate long-term effects.

The Kindness Campaign was started in 1994 under the National Program for the Study and Prevention of Youth and Family Violence at the University of Colorado at Colorado Springs as a primary prevention program to address the rising tide of violence among youth, in families and in schools. The Kindness Campaign is based on the idea that the best way to eliminate a negative behavior (bullying, put-downs, aggressive behaviors) is by focusing everyone's attention on the opposite of these behaviors: kindness. The program addresses each of the hidden elements of the culture of violence. The Kindness Campaign views violence as a systematic problem. It addresses the underlying causes of the culture of violence. Another goal is to facilitate a better understanding of the systematic roots of violence. One of the projects is to stage a play about the causes of violence that were present in the Columbine massacre. Through high school students performing this play and with the audience watching the play, the purpose is to raise everybody's awareness of the roots of violence. The campaign's co-sponsor, the local CBS television affiliate, conducted a random sample interview of its viewers in 1995 and found that 75 percent of its viewers believed it was having a positive impact on the community (Weinhold, 1999). Since then, the Kindness Campaign has co-sponsored many community events designed to build common ground and increase understanding and tolerance. These events include an Annual Interfaith Celebration of Kindness and neighborhood ceremonies to recognize the positive activities of residents. Kindness Campaign programs have been started in over 100 schools reaching over 70,000 students in Colorado Springs. Ten other cities have adopted the Kindness Campaign in their communities and schools. Goals accomplished include:

- Creating a positive school and community climate.
- Spreading kindness: a program guide for preventing peer violence in schools.
- Reducing bullying and aggressive behaviors.
- Dealing with student traumas.
- Addressing parental abuse and neglect.

The Nevada **Bully-Free for Me!** Task Force, which has as its goal the elimination of bullying in our schools, met for the first time in April 2001. The Task Force is a partnership between the Nevada Office of the Attorney General, Nevada Department of Education, Nevada's Teacher Association, Nevada Parent Teacher Association, Clark County, Washoe and Carson School Districts, members of the Nevada Legislature, and many other community-based organizations. Nevada Attorney General Frankie Sue Del Papa and Nevada State Superintendent of

Public Instruction Jack McLaughlin serve as the co-chairs for the Task Force. The task force has produced an Action Plan; a brochure describing the problem of bullying and what individuals can do to prevent it; created a Parent Tip sheet; is working to institute state and local conferences on preventing bullying; and is working to create videos and other materials for use in our schools to teach elementary age children about the harm bullying causes.

The **UIC (University of Illinois at Chicago) Police Department**, in collaboration the 12th District of the Chicago Police Department, has formed a partnership with four local elementary schools in Pilsen and on the West Side of Chicago. The purpose of the partnership is to examine and reduce bullying, intimidation and threats that occur in these schools and neighborhoods. The UIC Police Department has received a one year grant to conduct a study and use anti-bullying approaches in four elementary schools. The study consists of surveys created by the students with assistance from UIC researchers, police officers and school staff. This study aims to reveal and assess the perception and reality of bullying situations. Based on the results of the study, innovative approaches will be examined to include peer problem-solving forums, anger management, conflict-resolution training, and intervention training for school staff to proactively recognize and disarm bullying problems. In addition, training for parents will be provided so that they will learn to recognize behavioral indicators that may warn them that their children are being victimized or intimidated.

—— *What Happens If Nothing Is Done?* ——

Most people can see that bullying is not going to go away. If we fail to develop and implement effective intervention programs, bullying will clearly get worse. We will likely see the following:

- The dropout rate due to bullying will continue to rise (it is currently ten percent).
- The number of students afraid to go to the restroom at school will increase (it is currently 20 percent).
- The number of students staying home to avoid bullying will increase (currently, 162,000 students stay home each day because they are afraid to go to school).

- More short-sighted, reactive solutions, such as installing metal detectors, hiring more police to patrol the halls and putting in surveillance cameras, will be tried with no tangible results.
- More shootings will occur (64 percent of adults believe a school shooting will occur in their own community).
- The government will be forced to intervene and pass restrictive legislation holding schools and parents legally responsible for the destructive actions of their students and children.

Bullying is the most enduring and underrated problem in our schools today. Bullying is increasingly being recognized as having lasting effects on both the bully, the victim and the bystander. The effects of bullying persist into adulthood, with victims being at greater risk for depression, and bullies being at four times greater risk for criminal behavior.

The most important thing is not the action but the effect on the victim. No one should ever underestimate the fear that a bullied child feels. Therefore, it's very important that our schools work with students, parents and the community to eliminate bullying.

Chapter Five will provide useful solutions and strategies to the problem of bullying. Specific solutions will be provided for government officials, board of education members, law enforcement, school administrators, teachers, students, parents and the community.

Five

Solutions

Bullying, the combined use of power and aggression, is a problem throughout one's lifespan. Children do not just grow out of it. On the contrary, children who learn how to acquire power through aggression on the playground may transfer these lessons to sexual harassment, date violence, gang attacks, marital abuse, child abuse and elder abuse.

How do you feel when an adult comes up to you and says, "You look awful today. Did you find that outfit at a yard sale?" Now, as adults, we have the maturity and the right frame of mind to keep going and ignore the comments. We can reason that the person making the comments is having a bad day and taking out their frustrations on us. We can think of a lot of excuses for the person making the comments. However, it's different for children. Children are very trusting individuals. And why shouldn't they be? Since birth, they've been raised to believe that parents and adults are going to care for them. Protect them. Feed them. Clothe them. Give them the essential things necessary for them to be happy and content.

We need to protect our children, both the bully and the victim. The bully needs to be taught that it's not okay to hurt another child, and the victim needs to be taught that what one person says about them does not make it the truth, and it's not okay that they are being hurt like this. Let's not forget that children grow up. These bullies can only get away with their mistreatment of others for so long before it catches up with them. For the most part, adults don't take abuse for very long. Most adults will stand up for themselves. So if we allow our children to bully other children, are we unconsciously teaching and preparing them to do so in adulthood? If we just shrug off their temper and ill regard for their peers, are we condoning their behaviors and confirming that what they are doing is okay? If we are, then we've got trouble.

To stop children from bullying other children, it's going to take all of us working together. Each of us— teachers, principals, students, parents and community — are pieces of the puzzle that must fit together for the future of our children. This chapter will focus on specific strategies that each of us can adapt to stop bullying in our schools and homes.

Some children are more at risk of becoming bullies and victims than others, although this is in no way predetermined. It depends on a combination of individual, family, peer, school, and broader experiences. Understanding these contributing elements will help in developing solutions.

Factors That May Contribute to Bullying and Victimization

Individual Characteristics of the Child

Bullying: Difficult temperament, attention problems, hyperactivity
Victimization: Anxious temperament, social withdrawal, exceptionality

Family atmosphere

Bullying: Aggression within the home, ineffective planning, family stress
Victimization: Over-protective parents, family stress

Peer influences

Bullying: Aggressive peers, rejection, marginalization
Victimization: Rejection, isolation, marginalization, reputation

School Climate

Bullying: Ignoring antisocial behavior, inconsistent consequences
Victimization: Lack of recognition, communication

Many children may experience problems of bullying and victimization. For the majority (70-80 percent) the problems are minor and transitory. With minor intervention and support, these children's problems will improve. For some (10-15 percent), experiences of bullying and victimization may be more concerning and enduring. For a small proportion of children (5-10 percent) the problems of bullying or victimization are very serious and require prolonged and comprehensive intervention to support their adaptive development and to move them into a positive pathway.

How Do We Identify the Children at Greatest Risk?

The children at greatest risk of bullying and victimization can be identified by asking the following questions.
- Is the bullying or victimization SEVERE?
  Does it involve serious physical or verbal aggression?
- Is the bullying or victimization FREQUENT?
  Does it occur in this child's life?
- Is the bulling or victimization PERVASIVE?
  Does it occur in many contexts such as home, school or community?
- Is the bullying or victimization CHRONIC?
  Has it been a problem for a long period of time?

Bullying and victimization must be addressed from a systematic perspective. In order to intervene successfully to stop these problems, action must be taken at many different levels. Intervention must be implemented not only with the bully and victim, but also within the school, within the peer group (classroom and playground), and with parents.

Bullying and victimization do not occur in isolation. Therefore, interventions with the bully and victim are necessary but not sufficient. We need to extend our focus beyond the bully and the victim to include: peers, school, parents, community and society. To address the problem effectively, change is required at all levels of the system.

Implementing an anti-bullying program is a complex and prolonged process because of its systematic nature. Changes must occur with the bully, victim, peers, school staff, parents and community. A successful program must recognize the roles and responsibilities of bullies, victims, peers, teachers, counselors, principals and the community. And, unless the adults in the school change their attitudes and behavior, the students will not. Leadership is essential for change.

What Are the Solutions?

In order to effectively accomplish the goal of eradicating bullies and the problems they create, we must work together as parents, students, schools and communities. School bullying is everyone's business. It is unrealistic to expect it can be totally eliminated. We can't eradicate the conditions that turn our children into bullies and others into targets. But if everyone is concerned and truly committed to zero tolerance, then there is solid evidence that the amount and the severity of bullying can be reduced dramatically.

At the Government Level

Scandinavians were the first to study bullying; Sweden and Japan the first governments to launch anti-bullying campaigns after a number of youths in their countries killed themselves. The suicides prompted the government's recognition that bullying can have severe effects on a child's life, and moved them to take action to stop the abuse.

New Hampshire adopted an anti-bullying law. It calls for each local school board to adopt a policy that addresses pupil harassment or bullying. Any school employee who has witnessed or has reliable information that a student has been subjected to insults, taunts or challenges, whether verbal or physical in nature, must report the incident to the school principal, who in turn must notify the superintendent. The law leaves the remedy for bullying to the local school board.

Massachusetts set aside $1 million in federal funds to try to bully-proof its schools. Washington State's Senate voted to have its districts adopt anti-bullying and harassment policies, and Colorado is also considering similar legislation. Michigan does not have any statewide law regarding bullying but their state representatives still have an interest in pursuing this possibility.

According to one commentary,

> The push comes as many states and school districts around the country reconsider the problem of bullying. Recently, it was reported that Santana High [in California] had been battling a problem with bullying since 1997. The documents show four years before the shootings, 50 percent of Santana's students said they did not feel safe while on campus, 35 percent had been a victim of verbal abuse, and 12 percent had been physically threatened (1997). Accused shooter Andy Williams was described as a regular target of school bullies [Grabbing Bullying by the Horns, March 19].

We need to speak with our elected officials and share with them the problem of bullying in our schools and communities. In reality, our children are being denied the right to learn.

At the Law Enforcement Level

It's impossible for the law enforcement not to be involved with the issue of bullying. Bullying not only takes place in our schools, but a lot of times it carries over to our communities. Because of recent school violence incidents throughout the nation, police officers have become more visible in our schools.

The Halifax Regional Police Department launched Canada's first Anti-Bullying Hotline (1999). The officers saw more and more incidents of bullying taking place and believed these incidents were contributing to youth violence in the community (Goldbloom, 2000). A hotline was established so that students, parents or teachers could speak to a police officer quickly, directly and — if they wished — anonymously. Participating officers carry cell phones and students are provided with refrigerator magnets and book markers with the contact number. Phone calls are handled personally — never by an answering machine.

In Hastings, Minn., Prosecutor James Backstrom lays out one of the toughest juvenile justice policies in the nation. School bullies go to jail (Simon). If a child beats up another child, intimidates, harasses, or picks a fight on the playground or the bus, he or she is required to spend a minimum of one night in detention. One of Backstrom's goals is to stop bullying. Also, community service is part of the sentence. Children are forced to clean up a park or scrub windows at their school. Additional punishments might include writing an apology letter to the victim or attending counseling. This program has been a wake up call for children.

The Chicago Police Department's 12th District has formed a collaboration with four local elementary schools to examine and reduce bullying, intimidation and threats that occur in these schools and neighborhoods (UIC Neighborhoods Initiative, Spring 1999). The Police Department received a grant to conduct a study and use anti-bullying approaches in the four elementary schools. Students, with assistance from researchers, police officers, and school staff, are creating a survey they hope will help assess the perception and reality of bullying.

The results will help those who are involved develop such programs as peer-problem solving forums, anger management, conflict resolution, and intervention training for school staff. Training for parents will also be provided so they will learn to recognize behavioral indicators that could mean their children are being victimized or intimidated.

Australia has laws protecting people over the age of 16 from harassment and discrimination. For children under this age schools are legally liable.

SCHOOL RESOURCE OFFICERS

The concept of the school resource officer (SRO) was first initiated in Flint, Michigan, in the early 1950s. Since that time, a number of agencies have had school resource officers. However, the first formal program was initiated in Florida (Garrett, p. 65).

A major job responsibility of the school resource officer is to provide law related education and safety programs, one-on-one interaction, conflict resolutions and peer mediation for the students. These goals are met by having the officer teach classes in the school, work with small groups of children and be highly visible. The officer gains the trust of students and students feel comfortable talking with the officer about bullying and harassment.

Most states receive "code 69" or at-risk funds which can be used to totally fund the SRO's position. Other educational systems pay for the positions by local funds. In North Carolina, several SROs have been funded through the Governor's Crime Commission Grant — this pays for the position for two years, which would allow sufficient time to search for other sources of revenue (Garrett, p. 80).

Other assistance from law enforcement includes a strong DARE

(Drug Abuse Resistance Education) program in the elementary grades. A new component could be added to this curriculum and include bullying, harassment and mediation skills. Typically a DARE officer is selected from the police or sheriff's department and they actually teach 5th grade students once a week for 15 weeks.

At the School System Level

Local boards of education that haven't already done so need to explore the possibility of initiating anti-bullying policies in their school districts. These elected committees need to explore the research about bullying, then brainstorm and discuss possible solutions. They may want to consider the proposals of Common Sense Solutions (see Chapter 4), or they could:

- Identify programs and resources which provide information and training about bullying prevention and provide schools access to these resources.
- Provide assistance to schools in developing discipline policies consistent with violence prevention guidelines issued by the Federal Department of Education.
- Collaborate with the State Superintendents' Association, Principals' Association, Counselors' Association, and Teachers' Association in promoting the adoption of research-based bullying prevention programs.

The school district can initiate a whole-school campaign districtwide. This involves strong commitment and a willingness to work together on the part of everyone involved. It must involve all school personnel, other professionals as needed, students and parents. (These elements are discussed in Chapter Four, page 99 under the subheading "Steps to Successful Schoolwide Program.")

Michigan's State Board of Education created a policy that pubic schools and state education programs over which the State Board has policymaking authority should institute an anti-bullying program to promote a positive school atmosphere that fosters learning, and to create a safe and fear-free environment in the classroom, playground and at school-sponsored activities.

All members of the school system have roles and responsibilities in addressing problems of bullying. The extent of involvement of distal elements of the school system will depend on the severity, frequency, duration and pervasiveness of the problem.

At the School Level

Schools are getting more serious about the schoolyard bullying. Some of the recent perpetrators of gun violence, including those at Columbine, had been badly bullied in school, and they sought to get even. The best approach is a combination of adult supervision and intervention to change a school culture by teaching students how to deal with conflict.

Schools need to establish a social climate where physical aggression or bullying are not used to gain popularity, maintain group leadership or influence others to do what they are told to do. No one deserves to be bullied. Once the 60 percent of children who are neither bullies nor victims adopt the attitude that bullying is an unacceptable behavior, schools are well on their way to having a successful bullying program.

Schools need to advertise they have a zero tolerance policy for bullying, and they have a working anti-bullying plan in force. School faculty must maintain a high profile in terms of behavioral expectations of their students in order to gain support from the community and send a clear message to the families of present and future students that bullying will not be tolerated.

Once a school has established itself as a safe place for all students, school personnel will need to continually work at maintaining that reputation. It is a difficult task that requires the school faculty to put student safety at the top of their priority list. Remember, students who do not feel safe at school are unlikely to perform as well academically as they are capable, and their future opportunities may be impeded. A commitment by the staff to no bullying in the school must be a long term undertaking. When a new school year begins, staff should be sure anti-bullying policies have been included and discussed in the yearly goal setting process.

It's clear that what parents want most for their children is to know they are safe at school. When a child does not feel safe at school, it affects everything else that goes on in the child's life. Many schools have an unofficial reputation for tolerating bullying. This reputation is usually common knowledge throughout the student community. In these schools more children tend to feel anxious about their personal safety and as a result many are reluctant to attend. By the time a school has a public reputation for being a "tough school," many victims will have suffered in silence.

Faculty and staff can survey students anonymously to determine the nature and prevalence of the school's bullying problem, increase supervision of students during breaks and conduct schoolwide in-service training on how to implement an anti-bullying program.

A safe environment is one where students are not only free of physical threat but also free of emotional and psychological threat. The emotional harm bullies inflict on their peers is less visible, but not less real, than the damage done by weapons. As we have seen in the school shootings that have stunned the nation, children who are mercilessly harassed often become angry and alienated — sometimes to the point of exploding in lethal ways.

A SCHOOL IS LEGALLY RESPONSIBLE

Schools are ultimately responsible for protecting children, and they are culpable when they don't. Courts have handed down decisions awarding monetary damages to students bullied at schools, often after pleas for help fell on teachers' and administrators' deaf ears. In Washington State, Mark Iversen, a high school senior, had been bullied and harassed daily since junior high and finally physically assaulted in a classroom. The suit filed by his parents contends that the school took no action to stop the bullying because people believed he was gay. His mother repeatedly spoke to administrators at the school, with no result. As he progressed through junior high and high school, his grades declined. Finally, the bullying took its toll and Mark's parents sued the school system (Wall).

How effective is an anti-bullying campaign? Norway's program decreased bullying by 50 percent in the intervention schools over a two year period. This decrease was measured in physical bullying and in more covert behavior, like purposeful exclusion. The downward trend also occurred off school grounds, where students were unsupervised. Another finding from this program included a significant improvement in the school climate. Students had more positive relationships and a more positive attitude toward schoolwork and school (Wall).

A high school in Oakland put healthy relationships high on its list of priorities. Students have a consulting teacher they check in with twice daily. If there are any conflicts between the students, even a verbal altercation, they have to work it out before going back to class. The result: Zapata Street Academy's school climate actively promotes peace. Students will stop each other from fighting because they don't want any one person messing up a good thing (Wall).

PRINCIPALS

Principals set the tone for their schools. Bullying is reduced if the principal is committed to addressing bullying. Strategies used by principals include:
- Consistent and formative consequences for bullies;
- An open door policy for victims, with empathetic responses to their concerns;
- Working together with teachers on classroom management and strategies for troubled children;
- Reporting slips for reporting playground problems and or other non-supervised areas.

The key to reducing bullying in schools is a clear policy regarding bullying with consistently applied consequences.

For program development and evaluation, it is important to understand the nature and extent of bullying problems within your school. You can assess the extent and nature of bullying in many ways. The following are suggestions:

1. What happens and how frequently?
   - Distribute a bully victim survey to students, staff and parents
   - Make available an anonymous report box located in several areas of the school
2. Where does bullying take place on the campus?
   - Conduct an environmental assessment, know where and when the problems occur in your school
   - Draw maps of the school with the hot spots identified
   - Ask the staff to complete questionnaires
   - Create a bully locator map (all students look out for bullying and put a sticker on the map to indicate its location)
   - Have students do observations of bullying on the playground. Record what type of bullying it is and where it occurs

3. With students, follow up with an assessment of why bullying occurs more frequently in certain hot spots.

SAMPLE BULLYING SURVEY

Directions: Think about each question carefully. Put an X in the space that best describes you. Please do not put your name on the survey.

School_____ Date_____ Grade_____

This is how I feel about my school:

___very happy and good
___sometimes happy and good
___so-so
___sometimes sad and unhappy
___very sad and unhappy

This is how I feel in each of these places:

	Very unsafe	Kind of unsafe	So-so	Kind of safe	Very safe
in my classroom					
on the playground					
in the lunch room					
walking to and from school					
in the bathroom					
in the hallway					
on the bus					
at the bus stop					

How often have these things happened at your school?

	Every day	1 or 2 times a week	1 or 2 times a month	1 or 2 times a year	Never
teased in a mean way					
called hurtful names					
left out of things on purpose					
threatened					
hit or kicked or pushed					

Mark all that apply.

At school, who has:

        Boys and girls   Group of boys   A boy
           Group of girls   A girl   Nobody

bullied you   called you names
said mean things to you   tried to hurt you at school
teased you

In what grade is the student or students who bully you?

    In my classroom   In the same grade/different classroom
          Lower grade   Higher grade

When I am bullied, I:

____do nothing   ____tell an adult
____tell the bully to stop   ____tell a friend
____get away from the bully ____don't get bullied
____hurt other children

If you have been bullied, who have you told?

____my mother or father   ____another student at school
____my sister or brother   ____nobody
____a teacher or another   ____I've never been bullied
   adult at school

If you have been bullied, who has tried to help you?

____my mother or father   ____another student at school
____my sister or brother   ____nobody
____a teacher or another   ____I've never been bullied
   adult in the school

If you have been bullied, what happened after you told someone?

____it got better   ____I never told anyone
____it got worse   ____I've never been bullied
____nothing changed

How often do you hit, kick or push other children?

____every day   ____1 or 2 times a year
____1 or 2 times a week   ____never
____1 or 2 times a month

How often do you:
    Every day   1or 2 times a week   1 or 2 times a month
                1 or 2 times a year   Never
Say mean things
Tease others
Call other children names

How often have you seen someone:
    Everyday   1 or 2 times a week   1 or 2 times a month
                1 or 2 times a year   Never
Being teased in a mean way
Being threatened
Left out of things on purpose
Being called hurtful names
Being hit, kicked, or pushed

How often have you noticed bullying going on in these places?
    Every day   1 or 2 times a week   1 or 2 times a month
                1 or 2 times a year   Never
In my classroom
On the playground
In the lunchroom
Walking to or from school
In the bathroom
In the hallway
On the bus
At the bus stop

Who have you seen doing the bullying?
____both girls and boys   ____a group of girls
____a group of boys   ____a girl
____a boy   ____nobody

What grades are the bullies in?
____in my classroom   ____in a higher grade
____in the same grade but   ____in a lower grade
    in a different class
____I haven't seen any bullying

What is your ethnic group? (optional)

_____Asian   _____Native American

_____Afro-American   _____White

_____Hispanic

Are you a boy or girl?

_____boy   _____girl

Thank you for your answers.

Finding out how a school stands in relation to bullying is an important first step. The survey gives just some samples of the type of questions that teachers, students and parents want to ask. Some schools might want to ask others, but it's a good idea not to try to find out too much at once. After the information is compiled, it should be shared with the staff, students, parents and community.

The school staff is generally unaware of the extent of bullying problems. Increased awareness will increase the staff's recognition of bullying and willingness to intervene.

Educate the school staff about the definitions of bullying, the nature of bullying, the secrecy surrounding bullying, and children's reluctance to report bullying. Help teachers develop strategies to detect and intervene in bullying. Differentiate between rough and tumble play and bullying. Learn how to recognize power imbalance, which is sometimes subtle in bullying.

Bullying is less prevalent in schools where there are supportive relations among school staff, warm relations between staff and students, and shared decision-making among staff and students, and where adults do not model bullying for the students.

Schools that emphasize academics without respecting children's individual strengths and weaknesses tend to have more bullying.

Motivation and support from the school staff are essential. All school staff should be included in educational sessions. Staff, together with parent and student representatives, should be responsible for updating the code of behavior and its consequences. Teachers' attitudes are reflected in their behavior. When adults recognize the problem of bullying and their central role in reducing it, they supervise actively and intervene to stop bullying.

Parent meetings and newsletters should inform parents about the problems of bullying. Parents should talk to their children about bullying and be aware of signs of potential victimization. Communication between parents and the school is essential, as parents are often the first to know that their children are being victimized.

Peers play a critical role in bullying. Interventions must aim to change attitudes, behaviors and norms around bullying for all children in a school. Under the teacher's guidance, students can recognize the problem of bullying and their potential contributions. With the principal and teacher's support, they can develop strategies for intervening themselves or seeking adult assistance to stop bullying. Promoting attitudes in the peer group which support empathy for the victim and condemn aggression will reduce bullying.

Children involved as bullies or victims require individual attention. Talks with bullies should emphasize that bullying is not acceptable and point out the consequences in the code of conduct. If a group of children is involved in bullying, the bully and bystanders are brought to task. Talks with victims encourage them to speak up and confirm the school's intention to ensure they are protected from further harassment. Talks with parents to inform them of their child's difficulties is essential.

It's very important to establish a common philosophy on bullying among your staff members and teachers, and that counselors and psychologists are in agreement with possible standards and consequences.

To end bullying and violence, schools must send a clear message for a zero tolerance for harassment, put-downs and bullying. It's not possible for schools to eliminate cliques and differences among students. They can, however, demand that students respect one another, despite those differences, and treat every student with the dignity he or she has a right to expect in the school system.

To eliminate disruption, incivility and violence in the schools, the following strategies are suggested:
- Fostering social bonding and academic achievement;
- Promoting norms of nonviolence;
- Teaching skills for living according to nonviolence norms (skills include anger management, conflict resolution, and problem-solving); and
- Eliminating firearms and other weapons.

Parents must be partners in any effort to change school culture. The expectations of schools must be supported and reinforced in the family and throughout the community.

Conflict resolution skills—communicating, listening, and problem solving techniques—learned by all students will help change a school's atmosphere. If the school culture is one of civility and tolerance and one where emotions and differences are addressed, discussed and treated as problems to be solved, children will understand that teasing and bullying are inappropriate. Harsh punishment for bullies may just make the problem worse by making them more angry.

Children often bully others to increase their own power, or because intimidation and force are the only way they know to overcome obstacles. These are aggressive strategies, learned from observing others in our culture, like the adults around them or the people they see in the media.

At the same time, the fearful or passive victims need to learn to deal with bullies. Often victims of bullies can benefit from learning conflict resolution skills that will empower them, increase their confidence in their ability to handle a situation, and teach them to respond assertively, particularly in cases of verbal bullying.

Adults and children both should see bullying as a serious matter and respond to it, instead of ignoring it. That might involve a school appointing playground monitors—students trained to spot problems such as name calling that potentially could escalate. These students can identify behavior that many adults might not see and can support weaker students who may be victims. Sometimes they may act as mediators and encourage constructive solutions.

Everyone involved in the school—teachers, staff, students and parents—should recognize the problem as their responsibility. Taking a comprehensive and proactive approach to the problem can prevent more than someone losing his lunch money. It can prevent a tragedy.

General Principles and Goals for Schools

Checklist of environmental conditions that are needed for prevention to have a chance to work:

- Warm, positive and involved school staff.
- Firm limits on unacceptable behavior.

- Consequences are consistently applied when norms against bullying are violated.
- School staff must watch, monitor and intervene when bullying occurs. A clear and direct message must be sent that bullying will not be tolerated.

Goals for a preventive program should include:

- To establish a school Anti-Bullying Policy.
- To gain the involvement of teachers, staff and parents.
- To increase awareness and knowledge of bully-victim dynamics.
- To develop clear rules regarding bullying behavior.
- To provide support and protection for victims: help them to assert themselves, create opportunities for them to be recognized, and help them make peer contacts and learn how to manage and maintain friendships.

Effective school practices might include:

- A conference day to educate teachers, administrators, school staff, parents, students and community members about bullying behaviors, response strategies, and available resources.
- Increased supervision in the cafeteria, hallways, bathrooms, and on the playground, where most bullying behaviors occur.
- A coordinating group — typically consisting of an administrator, a teacher from each grade level, a guidance counselor, psychologist and or school nurse, parents and student representatives— to manage the program and evaluate its success.
- Ongoing meetings between parents and school staff.
- Discussions on bullying issues at regularly scheduled PTA meetings.
- Formation of a bullying prevention coordinating committee (a small group of energetic teachers, administrators, parents, counselors and other school staff, who plan and monitor the school's activities).
- Schoolwide events to launch the program.
- Parent involvement in school activities (highlighting the program at PTA meetings, school open house, and special violence prevention programs; encouraging parents' participation in planning activities and school events).
- Development and dissemination of advice and information pamphlets .

An effective bullying intervention program at the school level must do the following:

- Place primary responsibility for solving the problem with the adults at school rather than with parents and students.
- Project a clear moral stand against bullying.
- Include both systems-oriented and individual-oriented components.
- Set long-term and short-term goals.
- Target the entire school population, not just a few problem students.
- Make the program a permanent component of the school environment, not a temporary remedial program.
- Implement strategies that have a positive effect on students and on the school climate that go beyond the problem of bullying.

The emphasis is on preventing bullying, stopping it before it starts. In that way, educators hope to avoid further tragedies like the killings at Columbine High School.

Bullying behavior is evident even in preschool and the problem peaks in middle school. It's important that bullying intervention strategies be implemented as early as possible. Even if only a small number of students are directly involved, every student who witnesses bullying is affected. Even students who initially sympathize with or defend victims may eventually come to view bullying as acceptable if responsible adults fail to say otherwise. Over time, ignoring — or being ignorant of — bullying behavior will result in a social climate that fosters bullying, fighting, truancy and other social and learning problems in all students. The school has a responsibility to stop bullying behavior and create a safe learning environment for all students, a place where teachers can teach and students can learn.

Ensure that students understand what bullying means; what behaviors it includes; how victims, bullies and bystanders might feel; and what students should do when they or others are being bullied. Encourage students to discuss bullying behavior and teach them positive ways to interact with others. Listen to students' ideas about ways to deal with bullies. Take immediate action when bullying is witnessed or reported. Talk to the students involved, find out what happened and invite them to suggest ways to solve the problem. Take steps to ensure students and staff are familiar with school policy that addresses bullying.

At Central York Middle School in Pennsylvania, all students sign anti-teasing pledges and are taught how to appropriately manage their anger. Since this practice was started, the school reports a reduction in fighting. At Laurel Elementary in Fort Collins, Colorado, students undergo "Be Cool" training in which counselors present them with provocative situations and help them recognize the difference between a hot response and a cool response (Labi, 2001).

Next to parents, the child's peer and school experiences are most influential in affecting behavior and social growth. It is known that bullying occurs with greater frequency in schools where teachers are more tolerant of bullying behaviors. How can the time spent in school be better used to improve social awareness and social responsibility, and to decrease bullying and all of its consequences? Teachers are currently dealing with overcrowded classrooms, the integration of special needs students, shrinking budgets and, increasingly, a larger number of children with behavior problems. How can they adequately monitor bathrooms, cafeterias, hallways and playgrounds? Is it really the school's responsibility to be the source of discipline and social teaching, or is the responsibility better shared with the community at large? What about other students?

Students may well be the culprits, but they can also be part of the solution. Peer mediation and restorative justice programs involving students in monitoring and counseling their peers increase student responsibility, and can result in behavior improvement. A big buddy system where older students are paired with younger students who are having social problems could be developed. The older child could supervise the younger child and serve as a role model.

Early in the school year, teachers could develop sociograms within their classroom to identify the popular children and the social isolates. The children with fewer or no friends could then be included in supervised social programs at recess or lunch to help them make friends and avoid teasing. Each school should have a social worker, guidance counselor or a special teacher to oversee these supervised social programs and modify them to the unique needs of the school.

Bully or behavior boxes could be placed in different locations throughout the school. If a child is bullied, an anonymous note written by that child or anyone that witnesses the bullying could be placed in the box to be reviewed by the guidance counselor, social worker or principal. Students whose names show up frequently within the bully box would be investigated. Possible consequences could include assisting with schoolyard clean up, or preparing a written apology to the victim.

The same box could be used to report praiseworthy behaviors. This could minimize the negative attention to students who are observed putting notes in the box. Social awards and public praise could be used to reward these deserving individuals, and educate the entire student body about social skills and social consequences.

Parents need to be notified early if their child seems to be exhibiting any of several difficult behaviors, even if they are minor. Notification should not be for punitive damages; rather, it should be to provide an opportunity for parental teaching before there is an escalation of the situation.

Social awards for improved behavior, socially sensitive behavior, honesty and acts of kindness may be highlighted at school gatherings. Specific instances of bullying may be discussed at these settings to promote a wider understanding of how hurtful bullying can be. The notification and reporting of mean or hurtful behaviors should be viewed as positive acts that improve the school and help other students, rather than being perceived as tattling or ratting.

Teachers and principals need to realize that the school milieu, and services available to and for students, are confusing to those who are not in the system. When concerns are raised, they need to be seriously addressed, and not dismissed, ignored or minimized. Parents need information and to have options explained to them to determine the best solutions for their child's problems.

WORKING WITH PARENTS

Schools occasionally find dealing with parents of bullies and victims a challenge. It is essential, however, to build the links between family and school in order to support both the children who are aggressive and those who are the victims of bullying. The following are principles suggested for working with parents:
- Always contact parents and inform them of the problem;
- Convey the school's concern;
- Work together to gain understanding;
- Be supportive;

- Recognize differences in family values;
- Use a problem solving approach;
- Provide the school's perspective and school plans for monitoring the problem; and
- Invite future communication and collaboration in supporting the child at risk.

It's helpful for school personnel to consider the family circumstances that may underlie the child's problems of bullying or victimization. Often children who are experiencing difficulties at school are exposed to considerable stress at home. In working with children and their families, it is important to keep those potential stressors in mind. Stressors might include:

- Multiple hardships in a single family (financial problems, single parent stresses, illness);
- Lack of social support;
- High levels of parental conflict;
- Lack of monitoring the child's activities;
- Inconsistent and harsh punishment; or
- Low levels of communication and intimacy.

These are the things to consider when talking with parents of the victim:

- They may be overly protective parents.
- There may be a lack of independence in the family.
- Parents may be non-assertive.
- Family stressors (such as divorce) may play a role.
- There may be over-involvement by the parents.
- The victim may be the scapegoat of siblings.

COUNSELORS

School counselors can help create positive behavioral supports in their schools for students displaying pro-social behavior. They can advocate the implementation of a bullying prevention curriculum. Counselors can also:

- Work with students who bully and victimize others, individually and in small groups. These students need assistance if they are to become productive citizens. Early identification of, and appropriate intervention for, these students would go a long way toward helping them change these destructive patterns of behavior.

- Create groups with a common empathizing theme, such as children of divorce, and make sure to mix the popular students with the unpopular students in the same group to empathize with one another.
- Help communicate the message that bullying is not acceptable and all of the staff will help make it come to an end. Counselors can help teachers establish and enforce specific rules against bullying, as well as hold regular classroom meetings with students to discuss bullying and related behavior issues.
- Identify students who may benefit from participation in small groups where the discussion would focus on appropriate ways to deal with bullying.
- Model compassion for all students.
- Routinely ask children about school. Inquire about frustration from bullies or other sources of problems. Have they heard any name calling?
- When working with small groups, organize discussion topics to educate students about violence in schools and find solutions to problems. Plan interventions.
- Help set up a hotline for children to call about problems with students or teachers at school.
- Write articles or newsletters to educate the general population about the consequences of emotional and physical violence in our schools.
- Have a suggestion box in their office or classroom that relates to violence for students and schools, so students can make an initial complaint without the formality of an appointment with a school official, without feeling that they have officially informed on a friend or a bully, and without fear or threat.

At Junaluska Elementary located in Waynesville, North Carolina, the counselor meets with the teachers on a regular basis. During these meetings they decide which topics need to be addressed and the counselor goes into each classroom and conducts a lesson. These classroom lessons by the counselor occur every other week. The lessons are 20 minutes for primary grades and 30 minutes for intermediate grades. At the conclusion of each lesson, there is time left for questions or issues the students want to discuss. Also, the counselor has a box in his office in which students may leave messages about school, themselves or other students. The program has been very successful. Bullying and aggression have been reduced drastically.

At the Class Level

Teachers and other school personnel need to introduce and enforce classroom rules against bullying, hold regular classroom meetings with students to discuss bullying and meet with parents to encourage participation.

Rules should be brief and clear. Some examples might include:

1. We will not bully other students.
2. We will help other students who are bullied.
3. We will include all students in activities.

In all cases, students should be held responsible for their bullying behavior. It is important to remember, however, not to bully the bully, as this generates feelings of hostility and alienation. Immediate consequences for aggressive behavior and immediate rewards for inclusive behavior should be implemented. Possible sanctions include having the bully:

- Apologize;
- Discuss the incident with the teacher or counselor;
- Write a detailed description of what happened and have parents sign it;
- Pay for damaged belongings;
- Spend time in the office or another classroom;
- Spend time suspended from school;
- Lose privileges that are replaced with an instructive activity;
- Reflect on his or her own strengths and weaknesses;
- Role-play the victim of the same behaviors with the teacher;
- Observe acts of kindness around the community and identify the link between power (or strength) and kindness; or
- Lead a discussion on the harmful effects of bullying.

Teachers may also want to use a curriculum that promotes kindness, communication, cooperation, and friendship and includes lessons and activities stressing empathy, anger management, and conflict resolution skills.

Teachers could also have weekly meetings to communicate to students clear and consistently enforced expectations and to engage them as resources in preventing bullying behavior. They can establish good ongoing communications with parents by a newsletter, telephone calls or conferences.

Other effective strategies for teachers include:

- Serious talks with bullies and victims.
- Serious talks with the parents of bullies and victims.
- Role playing of non-aggressive behavior with bullies.
- Role playing of assertive behavior with victims.

WHEN BULLYING OCCURS

When bullying does occur in your classroom, the most important thing to do is react promptly, which gives the bully the message that aggression or bullying is not acceptable and will not be tolerated. The following strategies are suggestions for school staff in responding to bullying:

- Trust your instincts, use your judgment and follow through with one of a wide range of strategies from careful observation to immediate action, depending on the situation.
- Always approach and assess the situation (watch, stop it, talk to students who are witnesses, intervene, record, follow-up and evaluate).
- Beware of group dynamics that are likely to favor the bully.

There are many possible responses to conflicts among students, depending on the situation.

- If both sides are of equal power, then both parties receive equal consequences and the opportunity for mediation to solve their dispute.
- If there is unequal power, as in bullying, then the bully receives formative consequences and the victim receives supportive consequences.
- When a group of children is involved, even as an audience, focus consequences on the group.

INTERVENTIONS FOR BULLIES

As for their own efforts to deal with the bully, teachers may want to:

- Record the problem behavior and provide consequences.
- Educate the child about what bullying is and why it is not acceptable.

- Withdraw privileges and provide formative replacement activities.
- Determine ways in which this student can develop positive forms of leadership and experience power in a prosocial way.
- Assess the complexity of the bully's problem.

What if interventions do not work? Most students who bully are average children without major psychosocial problems. Situational factors are generally responsible for promoting their bullying behavior. The interventions previously mentioned are likely to bring these children into line.

If a student continues to bully in the face of these formative consequences, then there is likely a more significant problem. The following are suggested:

- If you have not contacted the parent for previous student incidents, contact them now. This is a good time to bring them in to help support the child. Carefully assess the parents' abilities to be supportive.
- Children who bully repeatedly, seriously and in different contexts require a behavioral management program developed in collaboration with a mental health professional.
- Given the systematic problem, the family may need help to support the student and to deal with bullying within the home context.

SUPPORTING THE VICTIM

When dealing with a bullying problem, it doesn't help to instruct the victim to solve the problem himself. Children who are persistently victimized have most likely exhausted their strategies for responding to bullying. Each time they have been bullied, they have likely tried something to stop it. By the time they approach an adult, they have likely reached the end of their tolerance because no strategy they have tried has been successful in stopping the bullying. Furthermore, peers consider it acceptable to bully someone with low social status. Therefore, it is essential that an adult assist the victim and intervene to shift the power imbalance between the victim and bully. The goal is to take the power to torment away from the bully and to protect and empower the victim.

- Reassure the victimized child that it is his right to feel safe at school.

- Assure the child that you view the bullying as serious and that his concerns and fears are justified.
- Counsel to support the victim in coping with the effects of bullying.
- Generate a list of possible responses that he could use if similar attacks occur. Ensure that the victim understands the importance of confiding in an adult if this form of harassment occurs again.
- Provide the child with language to speak out for himself. Empower him to speak out against his own victimization and that of others.
- Develop strategies to strengthen the victimized boy or girl. Build on his or her strengths to develop confidence. Ensure that he or she has others to support them and enhance their social status. This support can be built by connecting the victim with prosocial peers from his own age group; or having the victim buddy up with an older student in the school who can be a confidant, someone who can keep an eye on the victim, and who can start to rebuild the victim's social status.

CLASSROOM ACTIVITIES THAT
CAN HELP PREVENT BULLYING

To help students understand the feelings of others and make them feel good about themselves, working together is important. Teachers may want to try:

- Developing classroom rules with students.
- Cross-age projects.
- Cooperative learning activities.
- A class fundraiser.
- Community projects.

Teachers can work with students in class to develop rules against bullying. Many programs engage students in a series of formal role-playing exercises and related assignments that can teach those students directly involved in bullying alternative methods for interaction. These programs can also show other students how they can assist victims and how everyone can work together to create a school climate where bullying will not be tolerated.

Other useful components of any good anti-bullying program

would include individualized interventions with both the bullies and the victims, the implementation of cooperative learning activities to reduce social isolation and increasing adult supervision at key times (recess or lunch).

Promote a schoolwide anti-bully environment. Implement an anti-bullying campaign that involves the entire community, parents, students, teachers and administrators. Discuss with your students what bullying is, identify bullying and share personal stories and facts about bullying. Work with your students to develop classroom rules or procedures about bullying. Post signs designating and supporting a bully free classroom.

Know your goals. The first goal of all schools and classrooms is the safety of the students. The second goal is the level of confidence a student feels in order to report any bullying. In the beginning, middle and end of the year, administer a classroom survey about the problem of bullying. Share the results with your students and discuss solutions to any bullying problems identified in the survey. Instill, from the very beginning, a zero tolerance for bullying. It is important to insure a comfort level in the classroom and to respond to a report of bullying from day one.

Exercise the power of supervision. Provide students with increased adult supervision at prime bullying opportunities such as lunch and recess. Develop clear expectations used by the staff to promote consistency in the daily interaction with students and in their behaviors. Make sure everyone knows the expectations. When bullying occurs, call students to task immediately by separating them from the rest of the group.

Have a plan of action. Describe and discuss with your students the types and kinds of bullies. You may want to use statistics and read excerpts to your students. After discussion takes place on the topic of bullying, specify an effective plan to deal with a bullying situation, including consequences of the behavior.

Empower your students. Promote the welcoming of new students by demonstrating and role playing friendship skills. Provide various scenarios for students to develop the necessary skills to deal with bullying situations. Empowering students with mediation skills is very important.

Teachers may also want to:

- Integrate issues of bullying into the curriculum through activities such as drama, books, films, story writing, art and research.
- Discuss power and how it can be used aggressively.
- Highlight everyone's role in bullying.
- Create a supportive and cooperative climate to ensure students are not marginalized. Create a climate that permits and supports disclosure of victimization.
- Develop attitudes and activities that promote empathy for victims.
- Recognize and discuss dilemmas for peers.
- Differentiate between tattling and reporting.
- Develop language and scripts for intervening when you see someone being bullied.
- Teach skills for intervening.
- Have students keep journals. Writing is such an important way to connect to what's happening in a child's life. Children, through their writing, especially journal writing, will tell the teacher if they are experiencing a bullying situation.
- Read newspaper articles to students and allow them to bring in stories about fairness, and how people should be treated equally. Another discussion would be on how rejecting someone might have an impact on the individual.
- Engage students in discussions about the differences in people.
- Have children help each other academically. Children aren't likely to bully when they get to know the students.
- Teach respect and nonviolence beginning in the elementary grades. Nonviolence training conducted by older peers can be very powerful because younger students look up to high school students.

At Tuscola High School in Waynesville, North Carolina, students are buddied with an elementary school child. Students from the high school work with students not on grade level, those with exceptionalities and those with behavioral problems. It's a win-win prospect for all students involved. It allows the high school students to work with disadvantaged students and allows them to develop a tolerance for different handicapping conditions. For elementary students who are buddied, it allows them a role model, someone to discuss situations with and an academic tutor.

Community service is part of the curriculum at an alternative high school, Central Haywood High School. Students in grades ten, eleven and twelve spend one day a week working in the community. The school recently received the Governor's Volunteer of the Year Award. Students are involved in the following activities: delivering meals to senior citizens, performing yard work for disabled veterans, walking dogs, building a house with Habitat for Humanity and working at a daycare center. Through the community services, students learn to tolerate people with different abilities and backgrounds. The community service has had a great impact on the school — bullying is not a school problem.

INTERVENTIONS MIGHT PROVE BENEFICIAL FOR ELIMINATING BULLYING IN A COMMON LOCATION, THE PLAYGROUND

- Conduct an assessment to identify the hot spots;
- Increase supervision;
- Create organized play and supervise play areas;
- Be aware of groups of children coming together;
- For structural areas, develop a rotating schedule;
- Create clear rules and consequences; and
- Use conflict meditation.

At the Individual Level

At the center of any approach to bullying are those individuals most directly affected by and responsible for bully-victim situations— the students in the school. Most students are neither bully nor victim. They are, however, witnesses to the bullying that takes place around them. Students can promote a positive school climate by discouraging bullying behavior among their peers, promoting inclusion of all others in their activities, and seeking to foster acceptance of differences. All students need to be educated about bullying and what one can do if one is the victim of the bully and what one can do if one sees another student being bullied. To stop bullying, we have to empower our students.

There is a perception among some students that telling adults will not help because adult intervention is minimal, ineffective, and may cause the bullying to become worse. Some students do not report incidents of bullying because they fear retaliation. Often, a child sees the teacher as not interested in stopping bullying or only sometimes interested.

When children know that the school they attend actively works to make the learning environment safe, and that bullying is not tolerated, they can afford to relax their guard and divert their attention to learning rather than being safe. Even students who cannot be categorized as victims or bullies, but who witness bullying, feel more comfortable when they know that the school community, students, staff and administration stand together against bullying.

Adults should tell students, if you are being bullied tell a friend, tell a teacher, tell your parents. It won't stop unless you do. It can be hard to do this, so if you don't feel you can do it in person, write a note to your parents explaining how you feel, or perhaps confide in someone outside the immediate family, like a grandparent or aunt. Your class teacher needs to know what is going on, so try to find a time to tell him or her when it won't be noticeable. You could stay behind on the pretext of needing help with some work. If you don't feel you can do that, then go to the medical room and speak to the school nurse or the guidance counselor.

Try to stay in safe areas of the school at break time where there are plenty of other people. Bullies don't like witnesses. On the school bus, try to get a seat near the bus driver. If you have to walk to school and you're afraid of being ambushed, then vary your route and try to leave home and school a little later or a little earlier, or see if you can walk with other people who live near you, even if they're older or younger.

If you have a cell phone, be careful who you give your number to. If you receive threatening calls or emails, then tell your parents. It is a criminal offence to send offensive or threatening phone messages and if it continues, it can amount to harassment. The police can and do take action. Do not bring expensive items or lots of money to school.

If you see someone else being bullied at your school, tell someone about it. But don't get into trouble with the bullies; do it discreetly by telling a teacher when you get an opportunity and you won't be overheard. People who are being bullied need friends, so if you can help someone who is unhappy, please do so.

If you are being verbally bullied, laugh or ignore the comments or teasing. Bullies delight in you being scared and getting a reaction. Eventually they will leave you alone.

Tell the bully to buzz off or GO AWAY! Say it as angrily as you can and walk away immediately. Practice in the mirror.

Bullying is very upsetting and if you feel you can't cope, go to see your doctor so the problem can be officially recorded. A short course of medication might help. So might judo lessons so that you are confident you can look after yourself if necessary.

Being bullied is a lonely time and you might think you haven't got any friends. You may think you are the only one being bullied who has to spend break and lunch on your own. Keep your eyes open. If you see someone else on their own, try to start a conversation, about anything, school work, if you think you know their sister, if you think they might live near you, anything at all. Sooner or later you'll find a genuine friend who likes you for yourself. Sometimes bullies will take your friends away from you; perhaps your friends are afraid they'll also be bullied if they hang out with you. It's always very upsetting when friends turn against you.

Students can also try being a role model for others and do little acts of kindness, such as:

- Volunteer to help clean the room.
- Make a list of things you can do to bring more kindness to yourself, your family, neighborhood, or community.
- As you walk through your neighborhood, pick up any trash you see on the sidewalk.
- Send a letter to a teacher or other adult telling them what a difference their acts of kindness made in your life.
- Organize your friends to gather used clothing for homeless shelters.
- Make a donation to a local charity that is actively helping young people or start a fund-raising drive in your community for such an organization.
- Go through your toys and donate some of them to children who are less fortunate.
- Offer to baby-sit for a neighbor's children so they can take a break.
- When someone new moves into your neighborhood, visit them and welcome them to the neighborhood.

- When new students enter your class, make a special effort to get to know them and help introduce them to others.

ADVICE TO STUDENTS ABOUT BEING BULLIED

When you are being bullied:
- Be firm and clear — look the bully in the eye and tell him or her to stop.
- Get away from the situation as quickly as possible.

After you have been bullied:
- Tell a teacher, administrator or another adult in your school right away.
- Tell your family.
- If you are scared to tell a teacher or adult on your own, ask a friend to go with you.
- Keep on speaking until someone listens.
- Don't blame yourself for what has happened.

When you are talking about any sort of bullying with an adult, be clear about:
- What has happened to you.
- How often it has happened.
- Who was involved.
- Who saw what was happening.
- Where it happened.
- What you have done about it already.

HOW CAN YOU HELP A VICTIM OF BULLYING?

Do not join in if you see someone being bullied. Try to help the victim if you can, but do not place yourself at risk. If you do nothing, it implies that you think it is okay to bully and hurt others.
- Refuse to join in if the bully tries to get you to taunt and torment someone.
- Get a teacher, a parent, or other responsible adult to come help. This is not tattling. You are saying that you do not think bullying is acceptable and do not want anyone to get hurt.
- Try to get the child who is being bullied to tell his or her parents or a trusted teacher or counselor. Tell the victim that you will go with them to talk to an adult.
- Tell a trusted adult yourself if the victim is unwilling to report

the bullying. Do not let the bully know so that he or she does not become aggressive toward you.

How Parents Can Get Involved

Haywood County Schools, based in Waynesville, North Carolina, has a system-wide PTA/PTO organization. This committee has PTA/PTO officers from each of the 15 schools and they meet on a quarterly basis. The purpose of this group is to share good practices among the schools and to meet with the central office staff to discuss policies and procedures. At their last meeting of the year, bullying was discussed and concerns were shared. The group shared information from a bullying survey, which showed that bullying is increasing, particularly in the elementary schools. Also, 50 percent of the parents felt like their child had been bullied at school and especially on the playground and on the bus.

The group said the causes of bullying varied, but they felt like the following were contributing factors:
- Low self-esteem, lack of confidence;
- Patterning behavior from parents and older siblings;
- Lack of parental involvement;
- Lack of discipline;
- Lack of supervision in designated places such as restrooms, playground, hallways and bus; or
- That a child is different in some manner.

After a lengthy discussion on how parents can stop bullying, the following responses were unanimously supported:
- Talk to your child, stress to them how wrong it is to bully or use aggressive behavior.
- Talk to teachers about possible problems.
- Discuss your concerns with the principal.
- Teach your child how to deal with a bully and what they should do if someone bullies them.

The group felt very strongly about encouraging their child(ren) to become friends with other children. They also encouraged their children to join in adult-supervised activities both in and out of school. Inviting their child's friends to their homes was very important. This can lead to discussing school and getting a different perspective.

Other suggestions included:

- Write down and report all bullying. By knowing when and where the bullying occurs, parents can better plan what to do if it happens.
- Encourage children to develop new abilities and interpersonal skills, through such activities as team sports, music groups or social clubs. When children feel good about how they relate to others, they feel better about themselves and are less likely to be picked on.
- Talk with your child about what to do if someone is bullying them or others. Just telling your child to stand firm or walk away is not enough. For many victims, these skills do not come naturally.
- Help your child understand how bullying hurts other children. Give them real examples of the good and bad results of their actions.
- Help your child develop new and constructive strategies for getting what they want.
- Develop practical solutions with the school principal, teachers, and parents of the children your child has bullied.
- Tell your child not to cheer on or encourage a conflict between peers—this only encourages the bully, who is trying to get attention.
- Help your child support others who might be victims. Teach your child to try to include these children in activities.

A parental awareness campaign can be conducted during parent-teacher conference days, through parent newsletters, and at PTA meetings. The goal is to increase parental awareness of the problem, point out the importance of parental involvement for program success, and encourage parental support of program goals. It's helpful for families to become more involved in community activities and become friends with other parents. This allows parents to discuss joint problems concerning discipline.

HOW TO HELP YOUR CHILD

Behavior patterns begin at home. Teaching your child good communication and social skills at home will go a long way toward his or her success in school. Talk with your child. From the time children learn to talk, parents can have a running conversation with them about how their day went. This makes it natural to continue the custom after the child starts to school. Ask questions about their days. Ask about their friends. Get to know their classmates and friends. Volunteer your services to the classroom and school whenever possible.

Parents need to be observant of their children's behavior, appearance and mood, both for signs of the child being bullied or engaging in bullying behavior. Torn clothes, bruises, loss of appetite, mood changes, and reluctance to go to school are all signs that something is wrong. These are all signs that a child is probably being bullied. Many children fall deeper and deeper into depression as a result of long term bullying. Signs that a child is engaging in bullying behavior might be impulsiveness, showing no empathy for others, or a desire to be in control. Children who bully are often arrogant and boastful winners and poor losers when they engage in competitive games.

A child who has bonded well with his or her parents and feels warmth and caring from them is less likely to resort to bullying behavior with peers in schools and elsewhere. The parents should have also set adequate limits for a child's behavior at home and not allowed aggression toward siblings or other family members and peers.

The way a child is disciplined at home will establish a pattern for his or her interaction with other children at school. A parent who disciplines a child with yelling or hitting is teaching a child to react in that manner with other people. Often a child who exhibits bullying behavior in school has been the target of that behavior at home. Boys who observe their fathers handling disputes with a physical response or girls who observe their mothers practicing exclusion or manipulation of friends or family members will likely exhibit the same behavior in school.

Although the data show that both genders can engage in all of these behaviors, it also shows that boys are more likely to bully other boys physically while girls are more likely to bully with manipulation and exclusion or with spreading rumors.

Name calling is a favorite form of bullying among some children. Parents need to be particularly aware of the language children hear at home. Racial and ethnic slurs and name calling are another form of bullying. Targets of such name calling should be taught to look the perpetrator in the eye and tell them they don't like to be called names. They should be taught not to get into an argument or to try to change the perpetrator's mind.

Self-examination would be a wise course for a parent whose child has been accused of bullying behavior. The parent's first question, before taking action, might well be, "What have I done to contribute to this situation?"

Create a safe environment for your children to tell you about being bullied. Many times children are embarrassed to tell their parents what happened, thinking that their parents will blame them. Create an open line of communication by saying something like this: "Sometimes children at school pick on other children or say mean things to them. Does this ever happen at your school?" Reinforce the idea that if they are being bullied, it may not be their fault. Tell your child that the person who is picking on them has the problem, not your child. Bullies pick on people because they have problems of their own, not because of anything their victim has done. Don't teach your child to hit back or fight; it will only make things worse. Here are five steps that are good suggestions for a child who is being bullied:

1. Ignore the bully.
2. Move away.
3. Ask him or her to stop.
4. Tell him or her firmly to stop.
5. Tell an adult.

Notify teachers whenever an incident happens, and be prepared to be persistent until some action is taken. Ask the teacher: "Would it be possible to have the class get involved in a discussion about bullies, or to separate my child from those who are bothering him?"

If your child is unwilling to report another child's behavior to a teacher, offer to make the complaint yourself. Stress that it can be done in a way that is confidential.

When talking with your child(ren), it is important to have open conversations. Find a quiet time each day to review the positive and difficult aspects of their day. Questioning of children must be open and nonjudgmental. It is important that children feel accepted and loved, even though their behavior is displeasing and must be corrected. Positive behavior is encouraged and enhanced by positive reinforcement. Use stories to get information — when children are stressed and have difficulty talking about their experiences, it is sometimes helpful to talk about similar problems experienced by other children. Reading stories about children who have difficulties from bullying or being bullied helps children examine the problem and think about possible solutions.

Realizing that some children seem doomed to be victimized because of their nature or physical status, is there any hope of bully-proofing your child? Yes, you can help your child wear a psychic bully-proof vest to deflect the insults and physical abuse that bullies like to dish out. It's never too early to begin laying the framework for self-preservation. The following suggestions can assist you in providing a bully-proof vest for your child:

- Teach self-respect. A confident child is less likely to become the victim of a bully. A pat on the back or a positive comment can make a big difference to a child. Make sure positive comments are genuine. Avoid labeling or name calling that can make a child feel bad about himself.
- Let your child know it's okay to express anger or dissatisfaction. Don't chastise or stop your child when she's expressing an opinion. Show her that her opinion is valued — even if it means listening to a five year old argue vehemently about why she won't wear the pink dress to school. Letting your child stand up to you now and then makes it more likely she'll stand up to a bully.
- Stress the importance of body language. Verbally asserting oneself is not effective if one's body language tells another story. Teach your child to hold himself confidently, to bolster his assertive words by relaxing his body (deep breathing helps), keeping her hands steady, and maintaining frequent eye contact. Bullies tend to gravitate toward children who are unsure of themselves.
- Encourage friendships. Children who are loners tend to be more vulnerable to bullies. Begin early by helping your child develop friendships and build social skills. By elementary school, it may be more difficult for a shy child to make friends. Perhaps your child needs help in learning how to initiate friendships or join in group activities. It's also easier to participate in unstructured activities, such as playing on the swings, than to join in an organized game in progress.
- Teach your child to express himself clearly, yet diplomatically.

Help your child learn to use "I" statements. This form of self-expression works because it's indisputable and it shows how a child feels about certain things. When a child knows how to express himself without stepping on other people's toes, they tend to be popular with their peers, and having friends is a good way to keep bullies away.

Parents have the strongest influence in developing and teaching behavior, and conveying attitudes to their children. Each parent needs to recognize the social problems that occur at school and after school, and take measures to try and guide their child away from adopting the wrong group mentality. To achieve this, parents need to take the following actions:

- Recognize that even your child may be involved in bullying in social settings.
- Realize that all children can and do lie if they are scared of the consequences or are afraid that their behavior will disappoint parents.
- Discuss any reported behaviors openly, and not defensively, with your child's teacher. Work with the school to solve the problem; do not add to it. Denial does not result in solutions. Turn mistakes into teaching opportunities.
- Teach your child about bullying and have him or her look at things from the victim's side. Explain empathy to your child.
- Model proper language and behavior at home; your child is watching.
- Eliminate exposure to violent media. Children emulate observed behaviors.
- Do not buy toys or games of violence. Why teach your child to pretend to kill or hurt someone else?

What Should You Do If Your Child Is Bullied?

What should you do if you discover your child is being bullied? Consider telling your child about these strategies:

- Practice self-affirmation. One tactic is self-talk. Teach your child how to give themselves a pep talk. Positive self-talk addresses the issue of self-esteem. The better a child feels about himself, the less likely he is to be bullied.

- Know when to assert yourself. Put the bully on notice that this actions will not be tolerated. This can be as simple as telling the bully to stop and leave you alone. Therefore, your child should assert himself just once, and if it doesn't work, tell an adult.
- Don't encourage your child to fight with the bully. Normally, bullies tend to be larger. The bully's going to prevail. Such victories only encourage a bully to continue.
- Use humor to deflect the situation. Doing or saying something funny or unexpected is another effective means of deflecting a bully. Help you child develop some ideas to throw the bully off balance.
- Never let him see you sweat. Teach your child not to let the bully see him upset or scared. A child who is obviously anxious or tends to be sensitive — thereby letting the bully know his tactics are working — may need help finding ways to better hide his emotions.

One of the best ways to avoid being bullied is to avoid the bully. Suggest to your child that she take a different stairwell to her class in the mornings or take a new bike trail home. However, don't view running away as a long-term solution since it may only delay the bullying attempts. Rather, it should be looked at in terms of safety — a way to avoid immediate harm. Tell your child not to be ashamed to ask for help.

As a last resort, if the above solutions don't work, encourage your child to report the bullying to his teacher. Parents need to get beyond the misguided idea that children always need to solve their own problems, that it toughens them.

How Can a Parent Discourage a Child from Becoming a Bully?

Bullying behavior has many roots. There is no single cause. However, the problem is often triggered by something in the child's home environment. Their parents may be overly punitive or verbally or physically abusive, or they may be victims themselves, of bullying by a sibling or another child. It becomes very easy for a child to imitate what someone else does and what's been done to him, because he knows how it feels. Some suggestions for parents:

- Take a look at your parenting skills. Are you a bully at home?

Do you frequently criticize your child or demand unquestioning obedience at home?

- Watch your tone — and your message. It's important for parents and caregivers to examine their tone of voice when speaking to children. Avoid undue criticism. Children learn by example, and someone who is belittled at home may resort to such tactics when dealing with peers.
- Start to teach negotiation at an early age. The preschool years are the time to teach children to meditate their own disputes. With toddlers, parents and caregivers need to watch and intervene when trouble arises. Then try to move things from "might makes right" to a "let's make a deal."
- Don't be a wimp. Parents may also breed a bully by being overly permissive. By giving in when a child is obnoxious or demanding, they send the message that bullying pays off. Children actually feel more secure when they know parents will set limits.

It's important for parents to realize that all children have the capacity to bully. If your child is a bully:

- Make it clear that bullying will not be tolerated. Although it's important to determine why your child is behaving like a bully, emphasize that you won't allow such actions, and outline the consequences. If the problem occurs at school, tell your child you respect the school's right to exact punishment if it persists.
- Have your child walk in the victim's shoes. Since bullies have trouble empathizing with their victims, it's important to discuss how it feels to be bullied. How would your child feel if it happened to her?
- Help your child feel successful. It's important to emphasize your child's good points, so he can start to experience positive feedback (rather than negative attention). Is she good with animals? Is he a math whiz? Find opportunities for your child to help others, perhaps by volunteering to read to senior citizens, or helping a teacher after school. Doing good increases a child's sense of self-worth.
- Often children who are having a hard time relating to other children can learn some social skills with pets. Under close supervision, bullies may learn to care for and show affection to a dog or cat.

Although it might be unrealistic to expect that your child will never cross paths with a bully, it is possible to teach him the skills needed to avoid becoming the victim. Children who feel valued and respected and who have the proper weapons in their arsenal have the skills to withstand the slings and arrows the meanest bully dishes out.

Communities

Community resources need to be made available to the families of children who bully in order to help them develop a home environment characterized by warmth, positive interest and involvement by adults. Schools, homes and communities need to be places where there are firm limits to unacceptable behavior, where non-hostile, non-physical negative consequences are consistently applied in cases of violations of rules and other unacceptable behaviors, and where adults act as authorities and positive role models. Access to school-based mental health services would be very beneficial to the families of children who bully. Communities need to strive to meet the diverse needs of their youth.

Students who bully often need intensive support or intervention, so it is important for schools and social-service agencies to work together. Perpetrators are frequently from hostile family environments. They may be victims of aggression at home, or witness aggression among other family members.

In the school, children experience bullying as a frequent challenge. It is important to counter views that bullying is an inevitable part of the school life. The wider community, and particularly the adults within it, must take responsibility for making it clear that bullying is an act of violence and will not be tolerated in our society. Schools have an obligation to ensure they are a safe place for all children.

Help your community form a Family Violence Council composed of doctors, law enforcement, lawyers, child protective services and schools to intervene and support families. Adolescents are the vectors which carry violence from home into the community.

Community members can also:
- Invite an expert on bullying to speak at a conference or forum.
- Encourage civic and other groups to learn about their issue and see if there are ways they can help.

- Work with elected officials to celebrate "Respect for Everyone" campaigns.
- Invite parents and the community to "Teach-Ins' led by students, parents, and teachers to discuss strategies to prevent bullying on campus.
- Ask if you can become involved in service learning programs in schools.
- Encourage local television, radio and newspapers to cover anti-bullying campaigns.
- Schedule a Business Round Table with the chamber of commerce.

The way through the tangled jungle of violence in our schools can be found through education. Education of parents. Education of policy-makers. Education of children and education for our schools and communities. Without this education, our society is not going to get any better; bullying is not going to just go away.

If everyone works together to discourage bullying and respond to incidents, fertile conditions are created for students to develop a greater sense of connection to their peers and for seeds of respect and acceptance to grow.

Coming Together...

Now is the time to stop this. In the wake of school shootings and violence that our children are beginning to experience with other children, we need to make some serious changes. We have children shooting other children. Children shooting teachers and other adults. So, instead of standing around and ignoring the problem, let's become more pro-active and start taking control of the situation. How do we do this?

We need to treat our children the way we want them to treat others. It has to start in the home. It has to start with parents. It has to be spread to the teachers, and any other adult presence that enters a young person's life. We need to empower our children to think wisely, and to tread carefully and compassionately where others are concerned. Most of all, we need to be an example to them because they watch us all the time, even when we don't think they care. They do.

Next time you see a child hit another child or call him or her a nasty name, don't just shrug it off. Start now to protect those children from violence that can only hinder them in the future. We can do this, but first we have to choose to.

Conclusion

Public schools do not intentionally teach violence or promote aggressive behavior in children. School violence is a community issue. Research shows that communities with higher rates of violence (domestic violence, assaults, etc.) report higher frequency of school violence. If we accept this premise that schools are a reflection of their communities, then we must realize that schools alone cannot resolve the bullying issue. We need to promote the idea that there are multiple stakeholders involved in this issue and we are all in this together. The current research predicts a bleak future for children who bully and for their victims unless there are corrective actions taken by those in a position to influence their lives. We must always remember that this work is targeted at specific behaviors, not specific individuals. We must avoid labeling a child as a bully or a victim.

Bullying is a serious problem that can dramatically affect the ability of students to progress academically and socially. A comprehensive intervention plan that involves students, parents and school staff is required to ensure that all students can learn in a safe and fear-free environment. Children involved in bullying, whether as bullies or victims, may have negative attitudes, poor social skills and emotional difficulties which begin at home. These problems are transferred to the school and peer contexts, where they may be reinforced. The development of antisocial behavior problems depends on the interaction of individual characteristics and exposure to risk factors at critical developmental periods. Some factors within the child such as leadership, intelligence or resilience, or within the social system, can protect children from negative experiences. The problems of bullying and victimization are extremely complex. Consequently, interventions for these problems are also complex and should extend to all those involved: bullies, victims, peers, school staff, parents and the broader community.

The advice about dealing with bullying that adults give to children should always be sensible, realistic and appropriate. It has to be based on real experiences rather than untried theories. And, most importantly, adults should not make light of the problem or be patronizing in their attitude towards a child. A serious request for help deserves a considered response.

We must all be wary of only suggesting solutions which are based on our own experiences. Just because we have found things that work for us, this does not necessarily mean they will work for anyone else. Parents, teachers and children need to be given the option of choosing from a range of strategies. That is why much time needs to be spent trying to find out which strategies local authorities and schools, as well as individual teachers, parents and children, have found to be successful and which unsuccessful. Just as important is to understand why they have worked or not. Some strategies work in some schools but, because of human and organizational factors, not in others.

References

Ahmad, Y., and P.K. Smith. (1994). Bullying in schools and the issue of sex differences. In John Archer (ed.), *Male Violence*. London: Routledge.

Batsche, G.M., and H.M. Knoff. (1994). Bullies and their victims: Understanding a pervasive problem in our schools. *School Psychology Review*. 23 (2), 165–174. EJ 490 574.

Bitney, James. (2000) *No Bullying*. Minneapolis: The Johnson Institute.

Bowman, Darcia Harris. Survey of students documents the extent of bullying. *Education Week* on the Web (May 2, 2001).

Byrne, B.J. (1994). Bullies and victims in school settings with reference to some Dublin schools. *Irish Journal of Psychology*. 15:574586.

Bullying Prevention Program (Book Nine). Boulder: University of Colorado at Boulder, Institute of Behavioral Science, Center for the Study and Prevention of Violence.

Bullying widespread in middle school, say three studies. Site: www.apa.org/monitor/oct99/cf3.html.

Case law and settlements for school bullying. Site: www.successunlimited.co.uk/bullycide/cselaw.html

Charach, A., Pepler, D., and Ziegler, S. (1995). Bullying at school — a Canadian perspective: A survey of problems and suggestions for interventions. *Education Canada*, 35 (1), 12–18. EJ 502 058.

Child health alert: Bullying and psychological health in children. (October, 1999). Site: www.findarticles.com/cf_0/m087/19...le.jhtml.

Clarke, E.A., and M.S. Kiselica. (1997). A systematic counseling approach to the problem of bullying. *Elementary School Guidance and Counseling*. 31. 310–324.

Coloroso, Barbara. (2002). The bully, the bullied, and the bystander: Breaking the cycle of violence. Site: www.ctvnews.com/content/publish/popups/tagged/articles/coloroso.htm.

Craig, W.M., and Pepler, D.J. (1995). Peer processes in bullying and victimization: An observational study. *Exceptionality Education Canada*. 5, 81–95.

Crawley, Alvin L. Take bullying. *Arlington Public Schools News Check*. December 17, 1999.

Crick, N.R., and Werner, N.E. (1998). Response decision processes in relational and overt aggression. *Child Development*. 69(6), 1630–1639.

Davila, F. (1997). Boy bullied as gay sues Kent schools. *The Seattle Times* Web Archive.

Dickstein, L., and J. Nadelson. (1989). *Family violence: Emerging issues of a national crisis.* Clinical Practice Series No. 3. Washington, D.C.: American Psychiatric Association Press.

Dube, J. (1999). High school hell. ABC News.com, April 24, 1999. P. 1.

Espelage, D., et al. (1999). Interviews with middle school students: Bullying victimization and contextual factors. Presentation at the American Psychological Association Annual Conference, Boston, August 21, 1999.

Fried, S., and P. Fried. (1996). *Bullies and victims: Helping your child survive the schoolyard battlefield.* New York: M. Evans.

Garbarino, J. (1999). *Lost boys: Why our sons turn violent and how we can save them.* New York: Free Press.

Garrett, Anne G. (2001). *Keeping American Schools Safe.* Jefferson, N.C.: McFarland.

Goldbloom, Richard B. (1991). www.readerdigest.ca/mag/2001/10/bullying.html.

_____. (2000). Parents' primer on school bullying: If the school says, "We don't have that problem here," don't believe it. Site: www.readerdigest.ca/mag/2001/10/bullying.html.

Grabbing bullying by the horns. March 19. site: www.abcnews.go.com/sectionc/us/DailyNews?bullying010319.html.

Gregory, Melissa. (August 19, 2001). Bullying leaves emotional scars. The Town Talk Online. Site: www.thetowntalk.com.

Hawkins, D., Catalano, R., et al. (1992). *Communities that care: Action for drug abuse prevention.* San Francisco: Jossey-Bass.

Hoover, J.H., and Oliver, R. (1996). The bullying prevention handbook: A guide for principals, teachers, and counselors. Bloomington, Indiana: National Education Service.

_____, _____, and R.J. Hazier. (1992). Bullying: Perceptions of adolescent victims in the Midwestern U.S.A. *School Psychology International.* 13:5–16.

How to battle the school bully. Transcript: School Violence Expert Glenn Stutzky. (November 29, 2000). Site: ABCNEWS.com.

Jaffe, P., Wolfe, D., and Wilson, S. (1990). *Children of battered women.* Newbury Park Calif.: Sage. Site: Bullying for Parents and Teachers. www.lfcc.on.ca/bully.htm.

Johnson, D.W., and Johnson, R. (1995). Teaching students to be peacemakers. Edina, Minn.: Interaction Book Company.

Joyce, Greg. (2000). Teen found guilty in Abbotsford bullying case after friend committed suicide. Site: http://ca.news.yahoo.com.

Kumpalainen, K., Rasanen, E., and Henttonen, I. (1999). Children involved in bullying: Psychological disturbance and the persistence of their involvement. *Child Abuse & Neglect: The International Journal.* 23(12), 1253–1262.

Labi, Nadya. Let bullies beware. *Time* online. March 25, 2001.

Langer, (1999). Students report violent peers. ABCNEWS.Com. April 26, 1999, pp. 1–2.

Libaw, Oliver Yates. Standing up to bullying. Site: www.abcdnews.go.com/sections/livibg/DailyNews/bullying010307html.

Lienert, Anita. (2001). Schools wrestle with bullies. *The Detroit News.* Online site: www.ragead.org/headlines/march01,bully_25_print.html.

Limber, S.P; Cunningham, P.; Ivey, V.; Nation, M.; Chai, S., and Melton, G. Bullying among school children: Preliminary findings from a school-based intervention program. Paper presented at the Fifth International Family Violence Research Conference, Durham, N.H. June/July 1997.

Lindsey, D. (2001, March 6). Is there anything left to say? Salon.comNews. Retrieved from http://www.salon/news/feature/201/03/06/ school_shootings/ index.html.

Loeber, R., and Dishion, T. (1983). Early predicators of male delinquency: A review. *Psychological Bulletin*. 94. 69–99.

Marr, Neil, and Field, Tim. Bullycide *Death at Playtime*. website: www.success-unlimited.co.uk/books/bullycide.htm.

Maxwell, Gabrielle, and Carroll-Lind, Janis. (1997). http://www.nobully.org.nz/ bully-info.html.

Nansel, Tonja. Bullying is common study. April 24, 2001. site: www.abcdnews.go. com/sections/living/DailyNews/bullying010424.html.

Nansel, Tonja R., Mary Overpect, Ramani S. Pilla, W. June Ruan, Bruce Simons-Morton, and Peter Scheidt. (2001). Bullying behaviors among U.S. youth: Prevalence and association with psychosocial adjustment. *Journal of the American Medical Association*. 286, 16.

National Institute for Dispute Resolution (NIDR). (1999). *Conflict resolution education facts*.

Nolin, M.J., Davies, E., and K. Chandler. (1995). *Student victimization at school*. National Center for Education Statistics: Statistics in Brief (NCES 92-204). ED 388 439.

Noll, Kathy, and Carter, Jay. (2001). Taking the bully by the horns. site: http:// members.aol.com/kthynoll/myarticle.htm.

North Dakota youth risk behaviors. (1999). Bismarck: North Dakota Department of Public Instruction.

Ochoa, Julio. Kids get help conquering bullies. *Detroit News online*. Site: http://det-news.com/2001/schools/01/08/21/a01-272497.htm.

Oliver, R., Hoover, J.H., and Hazler, R. (1994). The perceived roles of bullying in small-town Midwestern schools. *Journal of Counseling and Development*. 72(4), 416–419. EJ 489 169.

Olweus, D. (1993). Victimization by peers: Antecedents and long-term consequences. K.H. Rubin 7 J.B. Asendorf (eds.) *Social withdrawal, inhibition & shyness in childhood*. Hillside, N.J.: Erlbaum.

_____. (1993a). *Bullying at school: What we know and what we can do*. Cambridge: Blackwell.

_____. (1994). Bullying at school: What we know and what we can do. Oxford, UK: Blackwell Publishers.

Paulk, D., et al. (1999). Teacher, peer, and self-nominations of bullies and victims of bullying. Presentation at the American Psychological Association Annual Conference, Boston, Mass. August 21, 1999.

Pelligrini, A.D. (1989). Elementary school children's rough and tumble play. *Early Childhood Research Quarterly*. 2, 4(245–261).

_____. and B. Bartini. (2000). A longitudinal study of bullying, victimization and peer affiliation during transition from primary school to middle school. *American Educational Research Journal*. 37(3), 699–725.

Pepler, Debra J., and Wendy Craig. (April, 2000). *Making a difference*. LaMarsha Centre for Research on Violence and Conflict Resolution.

Pitzer, Ronald L. (1992). Children's daily lives in Minnesota community. St. Paul: University of Minnesota Extension Service Research Monograph.

Prendergast, A. (1999). *Denver Westword*. August 5–11, 1999. 1–16. Site: westword.com.

Roedell, Wendy Conklin; Ronald, G.; and Robinson, Halbert B. *Social development in young children*. (1977). Belmont, Calif.: Wadsworth Publishing Company.

Salmon, G. (October 3, 1998). Bullying in schools: self reported anxiety, depression, and self-esteem in secondary school children. *British Medical Journal*. Site: www.findarticles.com/cf_0/m0999/n7...le.jhtml.

Sampson, O. (2000). Experts say bullying has dangerous consequences for kids. Knight Ridder/Tribune. October 31.

Saunders, C. (1997). When push comes to shove: dealing with bullies requires adult supervision. *Our Children*. March/April.

School violence: Bullying Site: http://privateschool.about.com/library/weekly/aa031901a.htm.

Serious bullying. ABCNews Commentary, November 24, 2001. Site: www.abcdnews.go.com/sections/2020/2020/2020_011128_bullying.html.

Shareef, Reginald. (2002). An ounce of prevention. Site: www.Roanoke.com/columnists/shareef/3891.html.

Simon, Stephanie. (2001). Bullies being sent behind bars: Policy calls for teens to spend the night in jail. *Los Angeles Times*. Concord Monitor Online. www.concordmonitor.co.

Straus, M., and R. Gelles. (1988). How pervasive is bullying outside of schools? www.balard.net/clients/weinhold/bully/pervasive.htm.

Study: Bullying common in schools. (2001). Site: www.catholicexchange.com/vm/index.asp?vm_24&art_id=6966.

Supporting schools against bullying: The second SCRE anti-bullying pact. Site: www.scre.ac.uk/bully/bullying.html.

Tizon, A. (1996, February 6). Sharp surge in teen violence puzzles town. *The Seattle Times*, pp. B1–B2.

UIC Neighborhoods Initiative: Building Partnerships for Stronger Communities and a Stronger University. New program helps prevent drug use. Spring 1999. University of Illinois at Chicago.

U.S. Secret Service National Threat Assessment Center. (October 2000). Safe school initiative: An interim report on the prevention of targeted violence in schools. Washington, D.C.

Vail, Kathleen. (1999). Words that wound. *The American School Board Journal*. September: 37–40.

Vossekuil, B., Redd, M., Fei, R., Borum, R. and Modzeleski, W. (2000). *U.S.S.S. Safe School Initiative: An interim report on the prevention of targeted violence in schools*. Washington, D.C.: U.S. Secret Service, National Threat Assessment Center.

Wall, Lisa. Bullying and sexual harassment in schools. Site: www.cfchildren.org/Pubully.html.

Walsh, James, and Khosropour. Paper presented at the annual conference of the American Educational Research. April 2001. site: http://ericcass.uncg.edu/virtuallib/bullying/1065.html.

Weinhold, B. (1999). Bullying and school violence. *Counseling Today*. 42(4) 14.

_____, and Weinhold, J. (1988). Conflict resolution: The partnership way in schools. *Counseling and human development*. 30 (7) 1–12.

_____, and Weinhold, J. (2000). Conflict resolutions: The partnership way. Denver: Love Publishing Company.

Westhead, James. (January 21, 2000). School for bullying victims. BBC News online. Site: news/bbc.co.uk/hi/englisk/education/newsid%5F613000/613102. stm.

Zaslow, Jeffrey. (2000). Tough kids, tougher calls. Site: wysi.html.

Index